Many Christians in Africa fa[...] and dine with small "gods" Monday to Saturday. It would appear the big God has prosperity but is hard to reach in the trenches of ordinary life without the help of small gods. Foster shows us that the God of the Bible is either God in all circumstances or not God at all. Believers have a privileged and rock-solid relationship with God, grounded in a binding covenant to be their God and believers his people. In fact, seeking after small gods separates us from the God who is always with us, in pain and suffering or in wealth and health.

— Rev Dr Aiah Foday-Khabenje, General Secretary, Association of Evangelicals in Africa

Whether you are trying to find the Way in life, wondering whether God cares about you, or bewildered by hard times, this book is for you. It shows how you have nothing if you are disconnected from God, but how through Jesus you have everything. This is wonderful Good News. I was blessed reading this book. I believe you will be too.

— Michael Cassidy, Founder, African Enterprise

Whether you are struggling with the question of belonging, feel unsatisfied with life, or have many "Why?" questions, *Highly Favoured* is for you! From the Scriptures and the ups and downs of his experiences, Foster shares that those who are "in Christ" are already "highly favoured" by God! The enemy tries to rob God's people of joy and hope by blinding us to this great truth. But whatever is happening in our lives, God has made an unconditional covenant with us, promising that he will be our God and we will be his people. Let this small book show you the big purpose that God has for your life – how you are already a part of the big story that God is writing!

— Dr Frew Tamrat, Vice-Principal, Evangelical Theological College, Ethiopia

Like a bright light, this book leads readers out of a prosperity gospel mindset and into the assurance of a life-giving relationship with God, rooted in covenant promise. Foster's many years translating the Bible give him deep knowledge of God's Word. His practical insights and personal experiences will enrich any reader who truly seeks assurance of God's favour.

— Rev Dr Joshua Bogunjoko, International Director, SIM

Highly Favoured could not have been written at a better time than this. Foster describes the struggles we face in our context when we are away from the soothing warmth of a relationship with the Creator. But God is committed to relate as a father to his people and to fulfil every promise he ever made, because he is God Almighty. This book will help you to reunite with the eternal source of salvation and refreshing revival. The Spirit of God truly leads you through the pages. I highly recommend this book to every person across Africa and the world.

— Pastor Jeffrey Muleya, Family of God Churches, Zimbabwe Tonga Bible Translation Project

Today people often feel driven to seek spiritual protection, power, and healing from ancestral spirits, spiritualists, and traditional deities. The tremendous appeal of material wealth, prosperity, and worldly success can overshadow the true meaning of the gospel of Jesus Christ. Drawing from decades of ministry in rural Mozambique, Foster explains why an understanding rooted in a covenant relationship with God is key to unlocking the true blessings and riches of Christ's kingdom, empowering believers to trust God through life's darkest moments by rooting their faith in God's sovereignty and covenant faithfulness.

This book is a must-read for any serious, thoughtful Christian trying to understand why God's promises sometimes seem to go unfulfilled, and why his promised blessings do not always result in worldly prosperity. It is a healing balm for spiritual wounds inflicted

through the hardships of life, and great restorative medicine for the Christian soul!
— Dr Nii A. Tetteh from Ghana, Assistant Professor of Medicine at Harvard Medical School

"God's Favour" is a frequent preaching and teaching subject in Africa that is often misunderstood. In this well-researched and carefully written book, Foster engages the topic in a fresh and balanced way that is both faithful to Scripture and meaningful to contemporary audiences. I highly recommend this book.
— Dr Clifton R. Clarke, Assistant Provost and Associate Professor of Black Church Studies and World Christianity, Fuller Theological Seminary

STUART J. FOSTER

Highly Favoured

OUR POWERFUL GOD'S COVENANT WITH YOU

OASIS INTERNATIONAL LIMITED
Satisfying Africa's Thirst for God's Word

INSIGHT
AFRICAN ISSUES
AFRICA'S AUTHORS
BOOKS

To my Sindia Jean

CONTENTS

Foreword by John Brown Okwii 2

Foreword by Augustin Ahoga 4

Introduction 6

Two Surprises 9

The Big Story 13

One Powerful Sentence 24

One Powerful Word 37

Four Marks of a Covenant 44

What a Covenant Looks Like 52

Does the Covenant Prevent Suffering? 60

Tied Forever to Jesus 77

It's Our Story Too 87

Postscript: A Very Big Question 93

Bible Study Guide 95

Something More 115

ACKNOWLEDGEMENTS

Many people have helped me write this book.

Meredith Kline and Gordon Hugenberger were teachers who shaped my thinking. For more than 20 years, the Elomwe translation team of Estevão Campama, Simões Duarte, and Zacarias Pedro have taught me, day by day, about Scripture, about Lomwe culture, and about living for Jesus. Hundreds of other Mozambican believers have shared their lives with me. Hannah Rasmussen and the team at Oasis have polished and shaped the book.

My wife, Sindia, has read every word and commented on many. Above all she has shared the living and the learning, each day, each year.

Thank you.

And thank you, Lord Jesus, above all.

FOREWORD

Having been involved in theological education for decades, I recommend this book very highly.

Rev Dr Stuart J. Foster is authoritatively qualified for the views he expresses in his book. His testimony of suffering and long-standing service in Mozambique shows he is a true missionary who has given his total life to Christ and incarnated into an African culture.

The author calls Christians to a journey of discovering our unlimited privileges in the covenant made in Christ Jesus. He clearly explains the marks of the covenant, which are hardly ever taught in most of our churches. As he explains them, the Bible passages used in the text become clear, alive, and powerful.

Today, some televangelists and preachers propagate the gospel of "name and claim it", that once one is in Christ there is no more suffering in this life. But Foster gives a balanced teaching about suffering, including a reminder that even Christ suffered as our example.

The book calls us all to stop depending on dead ancestors. We must trust in Christ because we who are born-again believers, God's people, now live in Christ, the Wisdom of God and the Hope of Glory.

You can read this book without a dictionary, teacher, or professor to help you understand it. Churches and secondary schools should get this book. It is a masterpiece for family development and discipleship.

I also recommend this book to seekers and backsliders. Welcome to the journey of self-discovery and renewal of God's covenant with you. Get the book and you will never be the same.

FOREWORD

Foster has dug the well from which many will drink to eternity. May God bless him and Oasis International for making this book available to the world.

Shalom!

Prof John Brown Okwii
Provost, West Africa Theological Seminary, Nigeria
Chairman and Professor Extraordinaire, Evangel
Theological Seminary Jos, Nigeria
May 2019

FOREWORD

Rev Dr Stuart Foster writes as one who has traversed many situations and lived experiences that have filled him with a passion to share his discoveries with audiences near and far. Here he beautifully retells God's great story, which transcends the traditional and the modern, focusing on the book's main theme – God's favour.

Life in contexts such as poverty, conflicts, and war can be terrifying and uncertain. Misfortune can seem to come from all over the place, whether from ancestral curses or our own self-created trials. People often wrongly seek to solve these dilemmas through human practitioners, who promise success through their rituals, or ancestors long physically dead. Born in Zambia to missionary parents and now living in Mozambique, Foster gives illustrations from his daily life in Africa of how people continually search for blessings and favour from unproductive sources. Examples such as the woman who can't find her bank card or the headmaster consulting a diviner across the river demonstrate that many Africans still search for blessing in the wrong contexts of African traditional religions. Even Christians who do not always rely on their faith in Jesus in times of crisis.

The truths of this book show that "traditional" world views do not alleviate poverty and suffering, and the promises of modernity and politics have not improved people's lives. Instead, the solution is found in God and God alone. His favour is enough for all. God's great story and covenant with us is the only way to access the blessings found in Jesus Christ.

Foster's book is both simple and complex. Simple, because he touches themes and relevant questions that one can find appropriate and relevant in many different cultures. Complex, because these are questions that the church in Africa is still working to explain, such as ancestors, curses, syncretism, and divination. This work underlines the need to deepen our understanding of these themes as we reflect on our relationship with God. For instance, Foster tackles the question of using intermediaries in order to access blessing, a problem that will remain as long as the priesthood of believers hasn't fully taken root in the church. Foster's work motivates us to accept God's high favour in our lives and embrace the grace that comes with it, building a foundation for the church and believers around the globe to grow upon.

My description, without a doubt, simplifies Foster's presentation. I hope you will read the text for yourself and discover God's high favour.

Dr Augustin Ahoga, Regional Secretary for Francophone Africa (GBUAF), International Fellowship of Evangelical Students

March 2019

INTRODUCTION

Perhaps your neighbours think of you as poor. You carry your hoe into the fields day after day, spending hour after hour bent over. Your hard work may bring a good harvest, if the rains and the seeds and the timing all go well, while the pests stay away. But then everyone else will have a good harvest too, and the price will be down when you sell your maize or your tomatoes. Maybe you, and your neighbours, think you are cursed.

Perhaps your neighbours think of you as rich. You managed to buy a small used truck from Japan. Every day you spend long hours at the wheel, hauling charcoal, oranges, or people. The traffic police always stop you to take their cut. Fuel prices are up. You may have a thick wad of cash at the end of the day, but you know that one breakdown or one accident could take away everything you have gathered. You paint a slogan on your truck: "God only knows." And you wonder. Some of your neighbours may be thinking of cursing you.

Time and again, from beginning to end, the Bible speaks about people who belong to God. It even talks about God belonging to us.

Life is hard. Life is scary and uncertain. We long for God's favour. We long for blessing. We fear the curses of our ancestors and of others. So we look for powerful people to show us the right things to do. They tell us about various ceremonies and prayers. Perhaps if we do the right ones in the right way, we will be favoured.

A woman went to the bank very early one Saturday morning so she would avoid the long queues at the cash machine. She needed cash for the next two days to get to a funeral. She had plenty in her account. But she couldn't find her bank card. There was no way to get the money out. She was upset. Even if she had millions in her account, it could not help her without that card.

I think that woman is us, the people of God in Africa. Our Father in heaven has put millions of blessings into our account. In Jesus, we are rich in his blessings. But so often we live as if we are poor. We are desperate, upset, and deprived. We don't even realize all the privileges we have or what our greatest blessings are. We can't find the card that will give us access.

Yet the Holy Spirit has put it right in our hands: it's the Bible. As we read the Bible more and understand it better, we can begin to stand tall in our blessings.

This is a book about God's favour. "Highly favoured" is what the angel called Mary when he announced that she was going to become the mother of Jesus (KJV). That is probably not the whole story of how she felt. For any mother, having a baby means joy but it also means disruption and pain. For Mary, without a husband, there was shame, too. Yet she was favoured, astonishingly, as no one else has ever been.

God's favour surprises us. It is surer than we imagine, as well as better – but also harder – than we ask for.

This book doesn't look to powerful or famous people around us. Instead, it looks to the Bible. What does God himself say about the favour and blessing he gives? Time and again, from beginning to end, the Bible speaks about people who belong to God. It even talks about God belonging to us: "You will be my people, and I will be your God" (Jeremiah 11:4 and elsewhere). This book follows that theme through the whole Bible, because the Bible really is a whole, not just a scattering of verses or interesting little stories that don't connect.

Jesus connects the whole Bible. He is the one who makes us a people who belong to God and guarantees us God's favour. He does it at the cost of his own life and makes it sure by his resurrection.

For more than 30 years, my wife and I have lived in northern Mozambique, a long way from the capital city. It is a very poor part of a very poor country. For the early years, we were surrounded by devastating civil war. We have seen people struggling for God's favour. And we have struggled ourselves. We have been gravely ill, time and again. Our middle child died of malaria just after her seventh birthday. We have also been deeply hurt, lied to, and rejected by those we thought were closest.

At the same time, year after year I worked through the Bible verse by marvellous verse, from the original Hebrew and Greek, with a great team. We wanted to help people who speak Elomwe have the whole Bible in their language and hear God speaking into their lives and needs. In the Bible I saw God's passionate, unrelenting commitment to his people. He is reliable in a world where nothing and no one else can really be counted on. I long for this truth to ground my life and the lives of people around me.

This book is born from both life in Africa and from Scripture, and from longing to have life in Africa and Scripture come closer together. My prayer is that it speaks to you and many others.

ONE

TWO SURPRISES

He was the headmaster of one of the best secondary schools in the nation. He was in a boat, coming back to the mainland from a small coastal island. But the boat was overloaded. It sank, and the headmaster drowned.

I asked, "Why did he go there?" He had no family in that area. It was a time of civil war. All travel was hard and dangerous.

It turns out that the headmaster (and lots of other people) had gone to see a famous *shehe* who lived on the island, a man known for spells of magical protection. He was able to sell powerful charms because of his contacts with the unseen world. But this time, the protection clearly didn't work.

Why would an educated, successful man, a secondary-school headmaster, make that trip? Why was he seeking protection? Why was he looking for help from the spirit powers? Some people might think that a person with that kind of position and intelligence didn't need anyone's favour. He could control his own life.

> In Jesus, we don't have to look for favour; it is guaranteed.

But many of us understand that we live in a dangerous world. All around us are forces we can't control and can't figure out. Human strength and human intelligence are useful, but they are never enough. We need favour, we need help, we need strength that comes from beyond ourselves.

Lots of people look for this favour anywhere they can. They go wherever they can find a specialist to help with contacting the spirit world. Maybe the specialist follows traditional religion, maybe he or she is a Muslim, maybe a Christian. All the specialists give people certain things to do, rituals to follow.

Other people are more careful. They want favour only from God himself. They look for favour only through the church. They perform duties and ceremonies that a good Christian does, following what their church teaches. If they do things right, these people expect the favour of God in their lives. In a crisis, they would not look for a *shehe* but instead try to find a pastor famous for his successful prayers.

Here are two great surprises from the Bible about the favour and help we long for:

**When we are in Jesus the Christ, we already
have the favour of God!**

**The favour we have is more wonderful (and harder)
than we can imagine!**

In Jesus, we don't have to look for favour; it is guaranteed. He secures our lives. We belong to him, in a deep commitment called a covenant. He is in fact our God, and we are his very own people, precious to him, with the right to call on his help. However hard things are, he has said, "I will take care of you" (Jeremiah 1:19).

The favour we already have in Jesus is also better than we thought and even better than we ask for. It may even be better than we actually want! Many times we look for health, for well-being, for enough or more than enough food to eat, for safe travel, and for our children to grow up well. God who made the very good world delights to give us these good things.

But when we belong to him, he wants much more for us. He wants us to be holy, to trust in him, and to have a joy beyond our circumstances. We can find our satisfaction in him and from him. He wants his glory to spread to the farthest corners of his world and of our lives.

This is a commitment so deep that it is scary. It will disturb us. It will rearrange our lives. It will hurt us in order to bless us. But the hardest part of all was experienced by God himself in Jesus: he died to fulfil his commitment to us.

In the Bible these two surprises are closely linked to one theme, a topic that winds its way from Genesis to Revelation. Usually, a big sack of flour for a bakery is closed by one thread. If you don't know how it works, it's a confusing zig-zag. You might get a knife and try to cut it, but that is slow and frustrating. But someone who knows how to open the sack simply grabs the thread at the right spot, pulls it, and the whole thread comes out. This theme, "You will be my people, and I will be your God", is like a thread interconnecting the whole Bible. If you know how to get hold of that string you will see the whole Bible opened. It will lead you to understand how to enjoy the rights and privileges of those who belong to God in the deep commitment of a covenant with Jesus. You will know how to live and work for him in this world.

I hope you will like learning about the Bible this way, taking one theme and following it from beginning to end. Together, we can see the wonderful unity of the Scriptures that is often hidden by their complexity. I am not saying that this theme of covenant is the only theme you could follow through the Bible. There are lots and lots of others. I am also not saying we will cover everything that has to do with covenant. This is just a beginning. I hope it challenges you to do more and better study than I have done!

In the next chapter, we will begin reviewing the panorama of the whole Bible, telling God's big story that is our very own story as well. Then, in chapter three, we will carefully grab hold of the phrase "You will be my people, and I will be your God" and follow it through the whole Bible. We will see that we really do have God's favour already.

In chapter four, we will stop to analyse just one word, a complicated word: *covenant*. As a Bible translator, I believe it is so rich that it doesn't come across very well in English. Chapter five will explore how God uses this word in an astonishing way: to tell us that we belong to him! Then in chapter six we will focus on a picture, an image, a symbol: the marriage of God with his people.

After that, in chapter seven, we will have to face a deep problem: If we really do have God's favour in this way, why are things so hard? Why does life hurt so much and so often if we are really blessed? We will find that our ancestors in the faith asked the same question and they can help us answer it.

The mystery of suffering points us, in chapter eight, to the one who suffered and rose again – to Jesus who brings the new covenant, marked by baptism and the Lord's Supper. Finally, in chapter nine, we will see the challenge and joy of living and walking in him.

By the end of our journey we will have a new confidence and power in our lives. We will know we have found favour. Different parts of the Bible will be more closely woven together for us. We will also see ourselves more closely woven to each other, to God's plan, and to Jesus himself. We will not need to scramble for favour; we will stand in it, strong and honoured, whether our neighbours see us as poor or rich.

TWO

THE BIG STORY

Have you ever stopped by a friend's house and found her already watching a television programme? Maybe it was a gripping story.

She invites you in and you sit down to watch too. But you don't know why the person in the story is so angry at the other person, or whether the next person on the screen is a friend or an enemy of the first person. They seem to be afraid of some terrible danger, but you have no idea what it is. Your friend is a bit distracted because she is so interested in the story. She gives you a word or two of explanation here and there. But you are left doubtful and confused.

For many of us, that is what it is like reading the Bible. Interesting characters come and go. The things that happen don't seem connected to each other. We don't follow the whole story from beginning to end. And we come away doubtful and confused.

That is not how it should be.

Our stories

We need stories to understand ourselves. We put ourselves into stories. When older people among Elomwe-speakers tell the stories of *namarokolo*, the clever rabbit, it is for fun, of course. It is also to teach. For example:

One day *namarokolo* heard about a party in the bush. It was just for animals with horns. But since he wanted to eat and drink with the others, he found some old horns and made some glue out of the sap of a tree. He glued the horns on his head, went to the party, ate, drank, and finally went to sleep. The sun

13

came up – and with its heat, the glue melted. The horns fell off. *Namarokolo* was caught, grabbed by his ears, and carried out of the party. His ears were stretched so hard that they have stood up ever since.

When we think about this story, it tells us that big and powerful people don't like to make room for little people. But a smart little person can take advantage of opportunities. Watch out, though! The tricks don't last for long.

Many other stories tell us something similar: We live in a dangerous world, but with clever ideas and with luck, we can accomplish a lot. After all, the *namarokolo* that seems so unimportant manages to have lots and lots of babies.

> When we find our place in God's big story, it becomes our story.

Other traditional stories tell us many other lessons. They teach that we need to respect our elders, that people we think are our friends can be dangerous, that we need our family. They teach that to really be a person, we need to fulfil our duties to the community. We need to have lots of children for life to continue in this dangerous world. We have to keep up the connection with our past. We may learn from our stories that jealous, envious people are all around us, eager to spoil the little that we have managed to earn.

As we hear these stories and tell them, a big, underlying story is being told. It tells us what is important and what we should do. It gives an overall view of the world, centred on managing to survive from generation to generation. The story tells of keeping society strong in a world of hardship, confusion, and danger. That traditional story answers the question: "How do we get what we need, surrounded by enemies on all sides? Who will help us?"

But that story can leave people stuck in poverty and suffering even as it tries to help them cope. If someone tries a new way of farming and it goes well, we may be suspicious: "That is not what our ancestors did! She must be using some magic so that she is taking from our fields to make hers prosper." Our envy leads to counter-magic and revenge when we might have learned a better way of caring for the soil.

Nowadays we still tell the old stories. We are still shaped by them. But there is also another big story and view of the world that stands out, insisting on being heard. It is not the story of tradition but of modern life. On television and all around us comes a clamour of little stories that tell this big, underlying story:

> We used to live in ignorance and poverty. We were enslaved by customs and rules that limited us, that kept us back. But the time of development, of progress, of freedom is here. Ignorance is evil, knowledge is good. Each one of us needs to find his or her way. We need to stand for our rights. We need to leave the past behind. With our understanding of science we are moving forward. Ignorance is in the dust. New things have come. Grab them. To the future!

We often hear people promising to change things in the world. At election time, politicians have an amazing list of new roads, bridges, hospitals, and schools that are about to be built. Every development project claims it will fix a social problem. Yet not all changes are for the better. We talk about development as if it were always good. But sin and evil develop, change, and adapt too!

In reality, the modern story often leads to unbalanced and even destructive wealth, with all kinds of new slaveries. People end up disconnected from each other and even from themselves, confused about questions of identity, wondering, "Who am I?" Sometimes this disconnection leads to arguments and even violence.

We need to be careful. The story and worldview of tradition is a mixture, just like the story and worldview of the modern world. Some good things are mixed with dangerous and confusing things. Great wisdom is needed to navigate our world and its messages.

In the Bible we have the story of God, his world, and his people. This big story is neither the story of tradition nor the story of the modern world. When we find our place in God's big story, it becomes our story. It helps us to understand the other stories and see what is wrong with them. Better than that, with God we live a life of favour and blessing.

God's story

I will tell God's big story twice, once in just four words (or so) and once with a few more words (but not as many as the whole Bible!).

Here is one way we can summarize the big story of the whole Bible: **creation, fall, Christ, completion**.

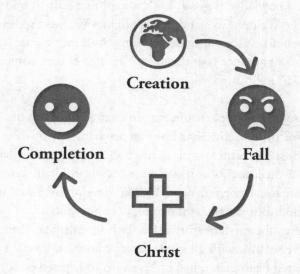

- God makes a good and beautiful **creation**.
- Mankind, put in charge of creation, **falls** into sin, rejecting God and ruining much of themselves and the world.
- But God won't leave things like that. He steps in, and finally, in Jesus the **Christ**, he deals decisively with the problem of sin and evil and begins to make everything right.

- At the **completion**, all those who belong to Jesus, along with a renewed creation, will be made completely good and beautiful forever.
- The first word, **creation**, answers the question: "What is it that God wants for us and for his world?"
- The second word, **fall**, answers the question: "What has gone wrong?"
- The third word, **Christ**, answers the question: "What has God done and is God doing about the bad situation we are in?"
- The fourth word, **completion**, answers the question: "What is going to happen to me and this world?"

This is the structure of the world's big story. We find ourselves in it. When we discover where we come from and where we are going, it will change the way we think and live.

My father was a physician and surgeon, usually very busy helping very sick people. But he would find time to plant a garden and care for it. I especially remember his juicy strawberries! He also liked to raise bees and harvest the honey. I can still picture him wearing a big hat, wrapped in a mosquito net as he went off to check his hives.

Although my father found peace and enjoyment in gardening as a hobby, farming for a living is very hard. Many times, the poorest people we know are farmers. Crops fail, animals die – and the people barely survive. How is it that farm work can be both beautiful and awful? Wealth and poverty are only part of the answer.

God wouldn't let his creation be ruined forever. He didn't abandon his plan to show his glory in his world through his people. A renewed world is coming and it will be ruled by a renewed people.

God's big story tells us that he delights in the fruitfulness, abundance, and variety of growing things, and we should, too. It also tells us that our human rebellion against God has infected the rest of creation. The wrong things grow, or the right things grow at the wrong time or in the wrong places.

Jesus often talked about raising crops and caring for sheep. Partly, it was so people could understand him easily. But it was also so we would understand that God cares about restoring the world. Creation is in disorder, but God is not leaving it that way. Jesus is putting it all right, starting by putting us right. And as we learn how to belong to him, we do our little part in putting things right. At the same time, we wait for God to finish his work, get rid of frustration forever, and establish beauty and abundance in all places.

What is true for farming is true for other kinds of work. It is true for other areas of life. The big story gives the shape that makes sense of our little stories.

Now I will tell this same big story in more detail, so we recognize the main characters and the main events:

In the beginning God **created** the world, and it was very good. He also created mankind, our ancestors **Adam and Eve**. He gave them the job of ruling his world on his behalf, showing how he rules and cares for the universe. But, encouraged by the great Enemy, they chose to be their own bosses instead of ruling for God. As a result, they lost their closeness to God. They spoiled themselves and the world in their charge.

God wouldn't let his creation be ruined forever. He didn't abandon his plan to show his glory in his world through his people. A renewed world is coming and it will be ruled by a renewed people.

But there needed to be another leader, like Adam, but one who would succeed and not fail. In the time of **Noah**, God used a great flood to wash the world's sin. Out of all humanity, only one family was left. But that wasn't enough to fix our problem. Neither punishment nor the threat of punishment fixed our problem.

Then God called one man, **Abraham**, and guaranteed that through him he would make a people for himself. God's favour was at work. This was going to be his channel of blessing for the world. Abraham and the people of **Israel** who came from him (by the power of God) were given a land to rule, just like Adam.

Years later, led by **Moses**, the people were saved from oppression and given God's law, so they would know how someone who belongs to God should live. They were to demonstrate God's glory on this earth in the land they were given. From that land they were to take God's blessing to all the peoples on earth.

But Israel behaved more like children of Adam than children of God. They kept on sinning. In this ruined world, they also had lots of enemies. Things didn't go well. God sent saviours, judges who were often like tribal chiefs, to rescue his people, but all the rescuers were flawed and weak.

Then God raised up a strong man called **David**. God made him king over his people. He used him to bring victories and rest from enemies. But David also forgot he was ruling in God's place and did not follow God's law. Things would have been even worse if it were not for the guarantee that God had given Abraham, which we call the *covenant*. God also made a covenant with David and guaranteed him a lasting kingdom through his descendants. He said that in the future, a king from David's family would bring true worship, leading everyone to praise and obey God.

The next king was David's son **Solomon**, a man of peace. He organized a temple, a place of prayer and praise to God. He made it beautiful beyond imagining with gleaming gold. But he also dirtied the great city of Jerusalem with forced labour, exploiting workers. He secured peace through political cleverness, linking himself to Israel's old enemy Egypt. As time went on, Solomon looked for help from other nations, other gods, other prayers, and other wives. David and Solomon and the other kings who followed them could only manage to create a shadow, a hint of the new creation to come. While the people and their leaders each went their own way, everyone still waited to see God's promise and guarantee become reality.

God sent messengers, called **prophets**, to get the people's attention. Time and again, it was as if God pleaded, *Let's sit down and
talk this through. We can call the village elders, we can work through
our problem. If I have let you down, tell me!* But, mostly, the people
didn't care. They kept up the ritual prayers and sacrifices, but they
showed by how they lived that they didn't really want to please
God. It wasn't the kind of behaviour that would give God honour
in his entire creation and among all nations.

God's favour is not something to abuse, to take advantage of. It
demands a response.

Still, in their failure God didn't abandon his people. He was
committed to restoring them. As the owner of the land, God took
it away from the people he had loaned it to. He sent them into
exile in Babylon as prisoners, to punish and teach them.

But that doesn't end the story. Some people repented and eventually came back to the land. And even before their **return**, God
renewed his covenant commitment.

This is how the **Old Testament** ends: a humbled people were
back in the land they had been given, but they were poor and col-
onized by foreign powers. Had God failed? So many times he had
promised a Saviour, a true King, a new Adam. But people looked
around and said, "Where is he?"

Years later, this is also how the **New Testament** begins. People
who trusted God had the same questions as before. The guarantees of the covenant didn't fit with the situation they saw all around
them. They thought, *God must be about to do something more!*
They expected that the owner who created this world was about
to act.

But what he did was a surprise. He sent someone called **Jesus**,
which means "saviour". People couldn't figure Jesus out. He was a
king, a prophet, and a priest all at once – but totally unlike the kings,
prophets, and priests that had come before. He called himself, more
often than not, the Son of Man or Son of Adam. In Elomwe we
could say *muchu-muchu*, the human-human, the human being who

is really and fully human. Jesus both declared and demonstrated that God was ruling. He showed the powers of creation made new. He spoke as God himself and as God's dear Son.

Jesus, the king, after confronting the authorities, let himself be captured, tortured, and **killed**. Dying in humiliation, he called out to God, asking him to show all people that he was the chosen one, that he was not a fraud, but God's true Son.

In Jesus' death, God's people wondered if God had failed. Jesus had said he was fulfilling God's covenant with his people and making it new again. Was it all for nothing? Had the Enemy finally won?

But on the third day, Jesus was **raised** from the dead. Transformed, he began to live a new life in his new body. It wasn't just his old life come back, but the life of God's new creation. God declared Jesus to be totally pure and confirmed that he really is the Saviour, King, Prophet, Priest, and Son of Man. He is the one and only Son of God. He is the Adam who succeeded where the first Adam had failed. God's favour stands on him and in him completely and forever.

It wasn't a defeat when soldiers killed Jesus by nailing him to a wooden cross. Jesus chose to take on himself the punishment of the first Adam, and our punishment as children of Adam. By his death and resurrection victory he guarantees and makes new the eternal covenant, a saved people who delight in God's favour. Jesus's resurrection is the launch of the new creation, for Jesus, and for the people who belong to him.

Indeed, God has never abandoned his plan to make a people of his own, who rule his new world in obedience to him, showing his glory by walking closely with him. There is only one completely faithful Israelite in the whole people of Abraham, and his name is Jesus. Through the power of the Spirit of God, Jesus is calling a new people of God. If we give ourselves to Jesus, if we give up other things we rely on for security and trust in him, we become part of the new people of God. We are welcomed, made part of his people, and begin to live a new life with him.

We become the new people who tell the world who Jesus is, that he is already ruling in the invisible presence of God himself. We share in his life by the power of the Spirit. People from all nations and languages belong to our new family.

At the end of this world, Jesus will **come back**. All enemies and all evils will be eliminated. Jesus and his people will rule the new world, the renewed creation, just like God wants them to. And God's glory will be everywhere.

This story makes me want to say, "Hallelujah, yes, do it!" It's my story. And it can be yours too. It's the story of God with his people. We now have the full picture, like the woman I mentioned in the beginning who watched the full television programme, not just a small piece of it. God's big story is the story that shapes how we read any and every part of the Bible. It shapes how we live, day by day. It tells us where we have come from and where we are going. And it helps us stand against the false stories that swirl around us and in us.

I once heard a preacher say that Jesus had come to give us a new list of rules – and if we didn't follow them, we would be in very big trouble. The preacher vividly described the trouble. But he didn't say that God or Jesus was doing anything beyond giving us rules and checking to see that we were following them. The preacher didn't fit what he said into God's big story. The hearers were left squashed and scared.

Suppose you plan to visit your family in a rural area. You find a vehicle leaving early, but after two hours, there is a problem with the axle. The fix only lasts for 30 minutes. You get into another vehicle, even though the first driver won't give back any of your money. Then you notice that your other money has been stolen. If you think like that preacher, you may decide that you have broken one of God's rules, so he is punishing you. Or you may think that one of your relatives along with the ancestral spirits wants to keep you from getting home, so your journey is cursed. Or, you might think that the government should improve regulation so that there is better maintenance of transport. And all of these things could be partly true.

But it would be better to remind yourself of God's big story and to tell God, "I don't understand what you are doing in this trip. I do know I belong to you and that in Jesus, you are showing your glory in this broken world, and that includes in this journey. Show me what to do that will honour you today."

> We belong to God, and he belongs to us.

In the next chapter, we will follow this whole story through a different lens, looking at one single phrase.

THREE

ONE POWERFUL SENTENCE

In my father's time, a lot of men were called "Bob". I can remember my mother saying "my Bob" to make it clear to everyone she was talking about her husband, not someone else. If you hear, "my John" or "my Mary", you know a mother, a wife, a father, or a husband is speaking. There might be thousands of other Johns and Marys out there in the world, but this is the one who belongs to me. The connection and the claim are strong and deep: "my" and "mine". In other languages, names are used less, but the possessives are still powerful: "my girl", "my boy", "my brother", "my man", "my wife". The "my" makes all the difference.

That is the way God speaks to us. Because of Jesus, God says to me, "my Stuart". He calls you "my daughter" or "my son". Because of Jesus, we also have the amazing privilege of talking that way about God and to God. We can say, "my God" and "our God". It is an astonishing privilege.

We have already looked at two surprises: (1) God's people are guaranteed his favour, and (2) that favour is so powerful that it changes us, transforms us. Both surprises spring from this deep truth: we belong to him, and he belongs to us. Time after time, from the first book of the Bible to the last, God's Word says, "**You will be my people, and I will be your God.**"

Quite possibly no other sentence in the Bible is so important and repeated so often. This is not one verse picked out and quoted on its own. It marks key turning points in history. Follow that sentence through the Bible, and you will hear the big story of the Bible.

It is the story of God, who doesn't stay distant from us, but comes towards us, looking for us. He is making and shaping a people who belong to him and giving them a wonderful job to do.

You may have heard this traditional African story:

> Back in the beginning, God lived near us. Heaven was much closer than the sky is now. One day a woman was pounding grain for her family. Thud. Thud. Thud. She was doing it so hard she made a lot of noise. She would lift the heavy pestle so high for each stroke that she would bump God. It bothered him, and he went far away.

There are many other traditional stories like this, but they all have the same ending: God went far away. It is a heart cry of our peoples: Something is wrong. God is not close to us!

The story of the Bible answers our yearning for God to be close again. God is making a people for himself, to be close to him, and he wants to include us.

The world has a lot of people – more than seven billion of them, in fact. All of them are made by God and given dignity by God. All of them deserve to be treated with respect. God shows all of them his goodness, power, and justice. But not everybody is called "the people of God". When we belong to Jesus, that phrase marks us out in a special way.

This chapter follows the sentence "You will be my people, and I will be your God" through the whole Bible, paying attention to its context each time. (At the end of this book you can see every time it is used, under the title "Something More".) These words are intertwined with the theme of covenant, which we will define and look at more systematically in chapters to come. What I want you to hear in this chapter is the amazing variety of ways it makes a difference when God says "my people" and we say "my God".

Being close to God changes everything. And we need the repetition. Let this truth go deep into your heart and settle there.

Let it weave its way into your whole life as it is woven into the whole Bible.

What about when God has still not done what he promised?

I will confirm my covenant with you and your descendants after you, from generation to generation. This is the everlasting covenant: I will always be your God and the God of your descendants after you . . . I will be their God.
GENESIS 17:7-8

God had called Abram to leave his country and relatives in order to channel divine blessing towards all the peoples of the earth. Abram trusted, obeyed, and went. But years later he and his wife still didn't have a child, let alone a whole people or the blessing for the whole world that was supposed to come through that child. Abram's faith wobbled. He tried to speed up God's plan, arranging another way to have a child, a son called Ishmael. But God made it plain that solutions are his business. They come from him, not from Abram or from anybody else.

Now in Genesis 17, God repeated what he had said in chapter 12, and already repeated in chapter 15. He insisted he would do what he had said. He added on to Abram's name (calling him Abraham now) as a sign that he would add to his descendants. God repeated his guarantee, calling it a *covenant*.

This commitment, God said, was to be reinforced by a sign on an intimate part of the male body, the foreskin. We will spend some time later looking at what the sign of circumcision means. For now it is enough to note that this is such a powerful symbol that many of our peoples have used it as well to represent maturity and growing up to be a full adult in society.

For Abraham, then 99 years old, and for his descendants, circumcised when they were only eight days old, this sign had nothing to do with maturity. It communicated something powerfully and directly: You belong to God. Don't forget.

And, eventually – several chapters later still, the promised child was born, the one called Isaac, the one who made them all laugh with delight.

We forget. God promises us blessing, and instead we see problems. He promises solutions, and things get worse. We say, "Help!" And he responds as if to say, *Hold this, here is my guarantee, wait. It's more important to trust me and be close to me than it is to see that thing fixed.*

(To read more on promises that seem late, see Ezekiel 36:28.)

What about when we are oppressed?

I will claim you as my own people, and I will be your God.
Then you will know that I am the Lord your God who has
freed you from your oppression in Egypt.
Exodus 6:7

Here, God was speaking to Moses about the people who had descended from Abraham. Blessing seemed a long way away. They were stuck in Egypt, oppressed by a wicked government. God had sent Moses to lead them to freedom.

Moses went, finally, after making a lot of excuses. He spoke to the Egyptian king, the pharaoh, in God's name. And then things got worse! So Moses complained. God's answer appears in this verse.

God cares about the cruelty, injustice, and oppression we suffer. But everywhere we look back in history and everywhere we look around us, we see powerful people taking advantage of the weak.

Moses had to use these words to assure the people that they

would be rescued from their suffering because they belonged to God. His commitment to setting his people free was so great that he had actually bound himself with an oath, calling down death on himself.

Moses was not entirely convinced that day. Still complaining, he did what he was told. And then, God demonstrated his power, utterly humiliating the world's greatest political and economic power of that time, along with all the spirit powers of evil standing behind it. (For another example of this, see Isaiah 40.)

He will do the same for us today.

What about when God surprises us?

> *You made Israel your very own people for ever,*
> *and you, O Lord, became their God.*
> 2 SAMUEL 7:24 (ALSO 1 CHRONICLES 17:22)

King David was stunned. At the beginning of the chapter, David had the idea of building for the Lord a house, a temple, a centre for worship and for sacrifice. The prophet Nathan thought it was a wonderful idea, but God didn't agree. Instead of David building a house for the Lord, the Lord would build a "house" for David! Not a building; God promised he would give David a royal family, a dynasty. God guaranteed that David would have a son who would rule after he died – which hadn't happened before in Israel – and a descendant who would rule the people forever.

David answered, "Who am I?" He didn't think he deserved the blessing he was receiving. He was amazed at the greatness and grace of the Lord: "How great you are!" He focused his wonder and praise and joy on the fact that the people belong to God and that God belongs to the people as well. (Psalm 33:12 does something similar.)

When I am blessed because I belong to God's people, when he surprises me with joys, "my God" becomes a phrase of wonder, worship, and awe.

What about when our enemies are winning?

O our God, did you not drive out those who lived in this land when your people Israel arrived? And did you not give this land forever to the descendants of your friend Abraham?
2 Chronicles 20:7 (See also Psalm 95:7)

In this passage, King Jehoshaphat, a descendant of David, was praying. Enemies were on the march, getting closer, so many of them that there was no way to compete with them in battle. The king organized a prayer meeting. He began to pray, talking of the power of the Lord. He addressed the God who rules all the forces, powers, and authorities in this world.

The king kept on speaking to "our God" about "your people". If God were weak, the king wouldn't have bothered asking for his help. But if the people didn't belong to God, there wouldn't have been any point either. Maybe he wouldn't even care about their troubles.

Jehoshaphat trusted that God was powerful *and* that he cared for those who belonged to him. So he explained the situation and presented it to the Lord: "We do not know what to do, but we are looking to you for help" (20:12).

Many times we confront enemies, both seen and unseen. They are stronger than we are. A demonized woman interrupts the sermon with curses. A judge imposes a crippling fine on our business. We don't know what to do or how to react.

But we can pray. As we pray, we trust that God will answer, will intervene, will defend us. After all, we are his people and he is our

God. Just like our father Abraham, we are his close friends. We have his favour and our enemies flee.

What about when we forget?

I am the Lord your God who brought you out of the land of Egypt that I might be your God. I am the Lord your God!
NUMBERS 15:41

The people and Moses had left Sinai. They had marched right to the edge of Canaan, the Promised Land. They had almost gone in, almost begun to enjoy the rich blessings of the land, when fears and doubts hit them. They disobeyed. So God gave them 40 years to wander back and forth from one side of the wild country to the other.

One of the many dangers during the journey, with all the work of daily life, was forgetting. So God helped them remember what he had commanded by putting little symbols on their clothes. The reminders would help them live as a people dedicated to God. A bit of fabric on the hem of their clothing pointed to a double reality, a double relationship: people with God and God with people. God didn't have them write some of his commands on their clothes. It might have been useful to have the ones they had just been disobeying. But instead, he pointed to the most important thing: to belong to him and to have him belong to us. (Psalm 100:3 does this too.)

The story is that the clever rabbit, the *namarokolo*, promised to make a magic potion to cure forgetting. He put some ingredients in the pot, stirred them, paused, then slapped his head, exclaiming, "I've forgotten the other ingredients!" So comes the proverb: There is no medicine for forgetting.

That is a problem for some of us more than others. But it is especially a problem for the people of God. We forget whose we are. We think we belong to ourselves, our homelands, our peoples, or our families.

We need to structure our lives with reminders of who we really are. And we need to renew our commitments, just as Israel did when the 40 years of wandering were over (see Deuteronomy 29:12-13). The reminders and the renewals are one reason that Jesus gave us, his church, the ceremonies of baptism and the Lord's Supper, which we will look at in a later chapter.

What about when we fail?

I will live among you, and I will not despise you. I will walk among you; I will be your God, and you will be my people. I am the Lord your God, who brought you out of the land of Egypt so you would no longer be their slaves. I broke the yoke of slavery from your neck so you can walk with your heads held high.

LEVITICUS 26:11-13

Freed, proud, standing tall. Flourishing, secure, close. The blessings of belonging to God in this chapter remind us of the Garden of Eden. But this same chapter goes on with dire warnings: What if, after all God has done for us, we let him down? What if we disobey him? Will he just walk away then? No. Because of the "my people/my God" connection, he will warn us, he will get our attention, and he will call us back to obey. God's favour is insistent, demanding. Leviticus 26 talks about God doing that over and over again. (The same kind of theme is in Psalm 50:7 and Jeremiah 7:23 and 11:4.)

Finally, at the end of the chapter, with the people still failing, still disobeying, we expect to read that it is all over. We expect God to say he can't take it anymore, that he is leaving this people forever.

That wouldn't be surprising at all. Obedience brings blessing, disobedience brings problems, and stubborn resistance wrecks everything.

But that is not the way Leviticus 26 ends. In verses 44 and 45 there comes a startling promise: After God takes away his gift, after he expels his people from the very land he gave them, there will be a "despite all this"! God will remember his covenant. He will preserve some of the people. The people have failed to keep their commitments, but God does not fail to keep his commitments. The father is still the father, no matter how rebellious his son. He wants to win his son back. So the people are not wiped out. (This theme also appears in Hosea 2:23.)

Leviticus does not say how God will do that; the rest of the Bible does. He will send his very own Son, Jesus, whose death will put sinners right with God once and for all.

What about when we want to fit in?

For you are a holy people, who belong to the Lord your God.
Of all the people on earth, the Lord your God has chosen
you to be his own special treasure.
DEUTERONOMY 7:6 (ALSO DEUTERONOMY 14:2)

After God rescued his people from Egyptian slavery, he met them at Mount Sinai to teach them about belonging to him. In a hundred different ways, their whole pattern of life was to show that God himself was a living, fiery presence among them. (That is the context of Exodus 29:45-46, where our phrase is used as well. See also Ezekiel 37:23.)

Years later, people needed reminding. All people are created by God and have some knowledge of him. They have differing traditions and customs, some good, some bad. But when we talk about the people of God, things are different. The connection with God is much closer. In the passage above, Moses spoke about God's "own special treasure", those who are most precious to God the owner.

When our son was very small, he had a little hat with a picture of a fish on it. He liked it so much that he didn't only use it when he went out of the house. He wore it in the house; he even wore it when he went to sleep. I remember one time when he woke up crying, "I lost my fishy hat!"

I showed him that the hat was right next to where he was lying. But he went back to sleep only when I put the hat on his head. The "fishy hat" was his special treasure. When it wasn't close, he wasn't happy.

After a while, the hat got a special smell – it smelled like our son. We are precious to God, and we are supposed to "smell" like him. When people notice us, they should notice something of the one we belong to.

This is hard, because people have all sorts of rude ways of talking about those who don't fit into their group. Some people think Elomwe-speakers in Ile district like to eat dogs, while most people don't eat dogs. If you call someone a "dog-eater", you have just insulted him. We don't like to be insulted, and we do like to fit in. So we wear what other people are wearing, watch what they watch, listen to what they listen to, tell ourselves their stories, and in time we smell more like they do than like God.

Watch out. This whole area is tricky, because there are plenty of false, twisted ways of seeming holy that don't smell like God at all.

It is also tricky because it takes time to become more and more like the God we belong to. The prophet Zechariah said it is like refining gold and silver (Zechariah 13:9). Gold and silver don't shine when they are dug out of the rocks. They have to pass through intense heat. This is the hard work that God does with his people, removing painfully what is worthless, the sin and evil that spoil us, so he can have a beautiful shining people. This, too, is part of the surprising favour of God.

We are God's special people. We fit into him; we don't fit into those around us. (In the New Testament, 2 Corinthians 6:16-18 makes the same point.)

What about when we need a new start?

I will give them hearts that recognize me as the Lord.
They will be my people and I will be their God, for they
will return to me wholeheartedly.
JEREMIAH 24:7

"But this is the new covenant I will make with the people of Israel
after those days," says the Lord. "I will put my instructions deep
within them, and I will write them on their hearts. I will
be their God, and they will be my people."
JEREMIAH 31:33
(SEE ALSO JEREMIAH 30:22; 31:1; 32:38; EZEKIEL 11:20; 14:11)

Most people can't ride a bicycle the first time they try. Most people learn by falling down, getting up, falling off, trying and trying again. Eventually they are riding. Even a small child can do it.

But a bicycle, no matter how hard it tries, can't turn itself into a motorcycle. It would have to be totally rebuilt. Someone would have to put a motor in it.

The Bible says that the people of God failed so completely to live like they should that only a new heart would do. For them, belonging to God had become just a set of rules. They would try to follow, they would fail, and they would give up. They needed a heart-level change. Only when God gave them a new heart would they be able to really live out the "You will be my people, I will be your God" relationship. And God committed himself to doing just that: making people change from the inside out.

The prophets promised it. Jesus does it. It is his death and resurrection that launches the new covenant and gives new hearts to those who trust him. It is the Spirit he sends that makes it happen. The letter to the Hebrews says that Jesus has dealt once and for all with all our failures. The promises are fulfilled (Hebrews 7:27; 9:12; 9:26)!

Do you need a new start? Maybe you have been trying and trying on your own, but belonging to God still doesn't seem real. Living God's way doesn't seem possible. Ask Jesus to give you a new heart, to welcome you into his new covenant.

What about when we are far from home?

I heard a loud shout from the throne, saying, "Look, God's home is now among his people! He will live with them, and they will be his people. God himself will be with them."
REVELATION 21:3

The fact is, we *are* far from home. We feel lost and vulnerable, like a boy from the countryside in a big city for the first time by himself. What are those lights at the traffic intersection? Which way do I go? Who can I trust? Who is planning to rob me? Things are not right in this world and we know it.

But that boy will feel different knowing that the auntie he loves is planning to welcome him and is already cooking a feast. We feel different, too. We are secure, because God is going to welcome us home. In Jesus, we are his family.

The last book of the Bible, the conclusion of the story, promises we will be home with God. In Revelation, John gives persecuted believers a vision of Jesus their Lord, fulfilling his plan in history and defeating all his enemies, seen and unseen. The vision then shows us a new heaven and a new earth, a renewed creation, the heavenly Jerusalem. From the conqueror's throne comes the great declaration, the final fulfilment of a promise made over and over again: God living right among us, we his people, he our God, at home. Ezekiel says it (37:27), Zechariah says it (8:8). Death, sadness, tears, and pain are gone. He has gotten rid of them. Everything is new, everything is good. What God has wanted ever since Genesis 1 is finally full reality. It is "mission accomplished" for God's people. They are with him, they rule forever, and they demonstrate his glory everywhere.

God makes a deep commitment, a risky and dangerous commitment, to his people in Jesus.

In Jesus, we are highly favoured by God, and this favour takes us all the way.

FOUR

ONE POWERFUL WORD

"How do you say, 'Good morning'?"

I might ask that if I am starting to learn a new language. If the language is Elomwe, someone could answer me, "*wooshishelo waphaama,*" which means "Morning is good" or "a good morning" – and which no one would ever use as a greeting.

Of course, the problem is my question. If I asked, "How do you greet someone in the morning?" I would learn something much more useful. In Elomwe, people say, "*Moosheliwa?*" which means literally, "Has the sun risen on you?" That sentence, of course, would not be a very helpful thing to say in English. There is no point in just looking for a word in a new language to take the place of each word in another language. That is not the way languages work. It's best to see how words are actually used by people in different situations.

God makes a deep commitment, a risky and dangerous commitment, to his people in Jesus. He gives us a guarantee of his favour. The Bible talks about this in many different ways, but the most important words in Hebrew and Greek (the original languages of the Bible) are usually translated *covenant* in English – which doesn't help us very much. It's not ordinary English, and it's a weak translation of a powerful idea. Learning how and why it is weak can make us strong.

So what is a covenant, and how will a better understanding of this idea change my life? I will answer these questions in two steps.

1. How might we translate the word *covenant*?

Suppose I told you, "I want to make a covenant with you."

You might be puzzled. You might wonder if I was joking. If you thought I was serious, you might ask to see the documents and look for a lawyer.

You see, we have a problem with the word *covenant* in English. Most people who speak English well could go a whole year and never use the word. Maybe nowadays it is some special kind of business contract? In the Bible, a covenant was solemn and important, but not really about business or lawyers. It was about the relationship between two people or groups of people.

> We are favoured, honoured, protected, and given power to serve God in his world.

There are some other English words that have been used to try to translate this ancient custom. I could say, "Let's have an **agreement**." The word *agreement* gets at the idea of two people or groups of people deciding to do something together but gives no idea of what they have agreed or of how solemn and important the agreement is.

I could also say, "Let's make a **contract**." That would mean that both of us agree to do something, and there would probably be penalties for not doing it. Our focus would be on what is to be done and not on who we are to be for each other. Usually, money is involved when we hear *contract*, which is not the Bible's point with *covenant*.

Bond has the idea of tying together. **Promise** makes a commitment for the future. An **alliance** commits two nations to fight together. All these are only parts of the biblical idea. They still don't tell me that I belong to you, whatever happens.

Testament is a legal word for an official document (a "last will and testament") declaring what someone wants done with his or her belongings after death. By tradition, we also use it for naming the two big sections of the Bible: the Old Testament and the New Testament. Unfortunately, this just complicates things. These testaments are not talking about someone's belongings after they die. They are talking about an original covenant from the time of

Abraham onward (the Old Testament) and a covenant made new in Jesus (the New Testament).

All these words in modern English mean very different things from what the original Hebrew and Greek words meant when they talked about the ancient custom of making covenants. Some African languages have expressions that get closer to the biblical idea. Many people groups in Africa have dances, ceremonies, or objects used to summon spirit powers and invoke their help, sometimes for good things, sometimes for evil. But it is hard to find modern words that speak of making a family-type relationship or that bring to mind the biblical idea of two people who belong to one another and now have to take care of each other. A weak way of explaining it makes it seem as if God's commitment to us is much smaller and much further away from us than it really is.

So, we will use the word *covenant*, but be aware that it has problems, just like any of the other words we might use. As we learn about ancient customs and how God uses them, the word *covenant* will get richer for us. This study will lead us into seeing ourselves as a special people, a family who belongs to God. We are favoured, honoured, protected, and given power to serve him in his world. In covenant, we also have very solemn responsibilities.

2. Why did ancient people make covenants?

In Africa we understand that life is about much more than me and what I want. People depend on each other and are connected to everybody else. If my nine-year-old son gets into a fight with a boy in the neighbourhood and hurts him badly, both families are involved. Fathers and uncles sit down and talk it through. Maybe the other boy is from a different language group, with strict ideas about honour and revenge. Maybe fathers and uncles are not enough, and leaders from both communities need to get involved. The groups we belong to matter.

The same was true in the ancient world: your group mattered. All over the world, the earliest societies were organized by family.

People knew they belonged to each other. They knew about honouring their ancestors. They respected the family hierarchy, giving first place to those who were older.

But as larger and larger numbers of people began to interact with each other, a family group needed some way to deal with other family groups. The easiest ways were fighting and stealing. People would justify their actions, as if to say, "Those people don't count as 'ours', so let's get rid of them, or at least take what we can from them. We respect 'our' people, not those 'other' people. They talk strangely, or do strange things with their hair, or eat disgusting things." This way of thinking is still common in our world!

But even pagans could see that fighting and stealing shouldn't be the only ways of dealing with other people. As time went on, people developed the ancient cultural custom of making covenants, which let people create new groups and work together. The custom of making a covenant could turn people who didn't count as family into family members. They would have the privileges and responsibilities of family. Covenants worked at the local level, joining individuals to the larger family group.

And as time went on, they were used for larger and larger groups of people. Covenant-making was used all the way up to international relations, the relationships between kings and peoples. Even at that scale, it did not lose the idea of family. When one king had more power than another king, he would be the "father" and the weaker king his "son". When two kings were equals they would call each other "brother". This had nothing to do with which one was older or younger.

What kind of relationship did a covenant create?

We can define the custom of covenant in the ancient world in this way: Covenant led to a **relationship** that had been **chosen**, that gave people **obligations to each other**, and that used **oaths so it would be guaranteed**.

Covenant customs made a **relationship**, a family-type

relationship. There were two parties, two people, or two groups of people, who would define how things would be between them. "From now on, we will be family." The relationship, the belonging-to-each-other, was the first thing. It was more important than what everyone ought to do or the duties and responsibilities they had to each other. This joining and belonging was symbolized by many different customs: by shaking hands ("Look, I don't have a weapon for attacking you!"), by eating together, by exchanging clothes. People talked about covenants using the language of relationship, of love and faithfulness and commitment.

> When we belong to each other, we have to care for each other.

But this family relationship had been **chosen**. The people involved weren't born belonging to each other. They weren't always family. There had been a decision, a choice, a ceremony with witnesses. Only then did the relationship begin. People who might have had nothing to do with each other now belonged to each other. Covenant customs created and established the relationship.

The relationship was not just a ceremony with nice words. Covenant brought **obligations to each other**. Nobody belongs to a family without some obligation or responsibility. Many times the obligations are assumed and don't need to be stated. But with our children we are often very specific so they learn: "You must sweep the dirt around the house each morning. You must wash up. Make sure that pot is clean. Stop what you are doing and greet older people with respect." There is a way of behaving and a set of responsibilities that go along with belonging to a family.

These obligations go both ways. They may not be equal, but they are there for both parties. A mother has huge responsibilities for her newborn baby. But the newborn needs to cry and take the mother's milk with all his might! In ancient covenants at the international level, there was often a document with a long list of obligations, stating exactly what each side committed to do for the other. A great king might commit himself to protect a weaker king. The little king would obey and not be late paying taxes. Obligations shifted according to the context of the relationship, but they were always there. When we belong to each other, we have to care for each other.

The commitment to a covenant relationship also used **oaths so it would be guaranteed** by the gods. Each party making a covenant would swear to keep their commitments to each other. It was not a merely private arrangement. In the oath, pagans would call upon the spirit beings, the gods, to step in to punish any faults and failures. Otherwise making a covenant would be like playing football (soccer) without a referee – not something you do in a serious game! Punishments were severe – not just a red card, not just suffering, but death: "If I don't keep this commitment, may I be torn limb from limb." Two parts of traditional covenant ceremonies made this extra clear: making sacrifices and a list of blessings and curses for keeping or breaking the covenant.

You couldn't really have a full covenant ceremony without sacrifices to the gods. Animals were killed, not just so there would be a good meal and not only to invite the gods to be present and witness the oaths being made. The sacrifices acted out in symbol what ought to happen to a covenant maker who did not keep his oath: he would be killed.

One ancient covenant document has a declaration by a king named Matilu. Grabbing the horns of an animal that is about to have its throat cut, he said, "This head is not the head of an animal, it is the head of Matilu." The animal's death represented the death of the one swearing the oath, if he failed in his commitment. The phrase translated "make a covenant" in the Old Testament is literally "cut covenant" in Hebrew. You made a covenant by cutting animals up in pieces, showing what should happen to the people making the oath commitment if they failed to keep it. In a symbolic way, a covenant maker said, "May I be cut up just like this if I don't keep this oath I am making." Making a covenant was dangerous! You did it at the risk of your life.

Ancient covenants often also had a list of blessings and curses. In some parts of the world people don't take words of blessing and cursing seriously. They are just nice thoughts or nasty thoughts. But traditional Africa is like the ancient world. We know better. People get very ill and even die after stealing from a farmer's field protected by a curse. I know of one man who earned money by crushing rocks by the side of the road and selling them to builders. He helped carry furniture for a pastor. The pastor thanked him and gave him a word of blessing. The day after he was blessed, he sold three times as many rocks as ever before. He went back to the pastor and asked, "Tell me about Jesus!" He became a believer because of the power of that blessing.

The list of curses and blessings in ancient covenants could be quite long, with more curses than blessings. The message was: "May the gods do all these good things (the blessings) to me and for me if I keep my commitments, and may all these other terrible things (the curses) happen to me if I don't keep my commitments." More good reason to keep your promises! Ancient people knew, just as we do, that it is easy to say nice things about caring for someone else. What is hard is doing what we have promised, especially when things don't go well.

All this cultural background goes before and behind the word *covenant* when we see it in the Bible. The word leads us into a world of customs and traditions with huge implications: social, political, economic, and religious. Covenants are about someone who doesn't count, who is a nobody to us, or worse, an enemy . . . someone our people have always despised . . . and that person is made into family, real family, not just pretend family. She belongs to us. He is ours now. This is someone with whom to share all we have, someone to fight for, someone to teach our ways. If we don't, all of us will be cursed. Doom will turn our greatest accomplishments into futility.

No wonder it is nearly impossible to find one English word to cover the whole idea!

FIVE

FOUR MARKS OF A COVENANT

I remember being nine years old and going to a new school. I had to start two days after everyone else. The school was not far from our house. But as I walked, it seemed very far. My feet were heavy and my heart was pounding. Which door should I go to? Who should I speak to? Everyone else would know what to do; they would see I was lost, and they would laugh.

Yet when we fail, God comes in the person of Jesus and takes on himself the curse we deserve.

But as I got close, another boy came up to me. A teacher had asked him to look out for me and to show me the way. Suddenly, everything was much better.

When have you felt lonely, scared, and left out? It is devastating to not belong. Yet the Bible says that is how we all start with God. We sin. We offend God. We resent him and want what we want. We are his enemies (Romans 5:10), with a father who is his enemy (John 8:44). We are left out of his glory and blessings (Romans 3:23).

Then, something amazing happens. He comes out to meet us and to welcome us. He not only shows us where to go and what to do, but he also says, "You belong to me. You are family now. Count on me." Our whole world is changed.

This is the story of covenant in the Bible.

In the Bible, people make covenants with each other. But surprisingly, God also makes a covenant with his people. The ancient pagans didn't make covenants with their gods. True, you needed the gods to make a human covenant; they were very much involved. But their job was to guarantee the promises and punish failure. They didn't make any commitments themselves. They were the referees; they weren't kicking the ball into the net.

In the Bible, God took something all pagans knew about and used it to talk about his relationship with his very own people. In using that familiar idea of covenant, he changed it profoundly.

Long before Jesus came, God did something astonishing: he made himself similar to a human being. He took the role of a person making a covenant. In the Bible he binds himself to people and makes them his family. He humbles himself to the point of making an oath. The God of life who cannot die says, in effect, "May I die if I don't fulfil what I have promised to my people."

At the same time, he doesn't stop being the God who demands that his people fulfil their oaths to him. Yet when we fail, he comes in the person of Jesus and takes on himself the curse we deserve.

For the pagans, it was impossible for a god to make a covenant with a human. But that is the astonishing story of the Bible: God making covenant and creating a people who belong to him, who are his family. When the ancient custom of covenant is used in this startling new way, huge changes follow. When we enter into this kind of relationship with God himself, we see the world and understand reality very differently. Our relationship with him is:

- exclusive,
- secure,
- demanding, and
- full of purpose.

Let's look more closely at those four marks.

Exclusive

A covenant relationship with God is exclusive. It leaves no room for relationships with other gods or spirit powers.

Maybe we assume that everybody today knows there is only one

God, who made the world. But in the ancient world, things were very different. (Or maybe not so different?) People understood the world to be full of unseen powers, spirits with a massive impact on people's lives, for good or for harm. Anyone who didn't manage to get the help and favour of these powers was in danger. The different gods, it was thought, specialized in different things: some were expert at war, some gave health, some were for travellers, some helped the household home, some helped in giving birth, some gave farmers success. Similarly, in Lomwe tradition, hunting is a spiritual challenge. Before and after confronting the dangers of the bush and wild animals, hunters performed a careful series of rituals and ceremonies to make sure the ancestral spirits would help them and protect them from the spirits of the wilderness.

But in the Bible, God makes a covenant with his people. He basically says: "You belong to me. I belong to you. I made the world. All your worries, all your problems – bring them to me. Don't have anything more to do with those other spirits, those so-called gods. They aren't authorized to mess with you. I am the one with solutions for you."

Covenant means that God and his people belong to each other. There is no room in that relationship for other spirit powers or anything else to be treated like a god. People in God's family don't go elsewhere to find solutions to their problems. They ask their Father. If you need help with your daughter's school fees, you don't start by asking a stranger for help. When your son gets in trouble with the police, you call the family together for help.

God is family now. It offends him when we strap a protecting charm around our baby's belly, as if God doesn't care. The first commandment of the ten says: "You must not have any other god but me" (Exodus 20:3). According to Jesus, the first commandment of the two great ones is: "Love the Lord your God with all your heart, all your soul, and all your strength" (Deuteronomy 6:5). There is no space for loyalty to any other spiritual power.

Even today, this covenant challenges us. Most people see

religion as a means to get God's help for the problems of life. They look for favour from on high. If they do the things expected of them (as explained by the religion they follow), God will do something for them. If they also look for help from other spirit powers, they assume that counts, too.

But through his covenant God reminds us: *Don't look for solutions; look to me. Only in me will you find solutions for everything.* In the Bible, covenant creates an exclusive relationship with God.

An exclusive relationship is not always easy. One friend, Pastor Ntikwa, kept having sugar cane stolen from his plot along the stream bed. The sugar cane in the sections upstream and downstream from him were not being touched. I asked him, "Why do they steal only yours?"

He said, "Everyone knows I'm a pastor, so I don't put spells on my crop. Someone who steals from my neighbours will get sick, but no one is afraid of stealing from me!" He counted on God to take care of him, even though everyone thought he was foolish, and even though he lost a lot of sugar cane.

> But in the covenant, God who commands the world creates obligations for himself.

Later, as he continued trusting God, Pastor Ntikwa was given a motorbike through his church to help with his ministry. Ten times his whole crop of sugar cane could never have paid for such a gift.

As Christians, people should know we will have nothing to do with spells and the spirits. God promises to take care of us, but we must trust him alone.

Secure

This relationship with God is also secure. It comes into our lives with God's guarantee. It brings the surprise that we already have his favour and that his favour is not going away.

Outside the covenant, others know that God is powerful. He can do anything.

Still, we might ask, "But what is he going to do? What if someone else comes along and messes up what he has done? What if he goes away from us?" We humans are full of doubt, from ancient times until today. We are fragile, and the world is full of danger.

But in the covenant, God who commands the world creates obligations for himself. He must take care of his people; he swore an oath that he would. To his own people, he guarantees life, not death. His promise is clear: "I will never fail you. I will never abandon you" (Hebrews 13:5), renewing the promise he made long before: "The Lord will personally go ahead of you. He will be with you; he will neither fail you nor abandon you" (Deuteronomy 31:8). Jesus makes the same kind of promise, to care for us and to guard us, calling us his sheep: "No one can snatch them away from me" (John 10:28).

This doesn't mean that everything goes just as we want it to in the world. No. Pastor Ntikwa's sugar cane was still stolen. It hurt. It was hard for him to trust. Yet God's covenant promise means that when things don't go as we hoped, although we may doubt and complain, we are still secure. God has given us his guarantee. He is concerned about us, more concerned than we are about ourselves. We don't manipulate him to get his favour.

We are okay.

We are safe.

We are in him.

We belong to him.

Demanding

A covenant relationship with God is also demanding. It creates obligations, for him and for us. We belong to each other and cannot abandon each other.

My wife and I have friends who adopted a war orphan when he was five years old. He had learned to steal food and to lie in order to survive. He hated following rules. It took many months for him to realize that there would be food for him at mealtimes, every day.

He had to learn that he did not need to grab or steal, because it would be given to him. He would be given not exactly what he wanted, but what he needed to grow strong. Eventually he learned to ask for what he needed and to receive it with respect. He belonged. He was cared for. He needed to behave like a member of the family.

In the covenant, God takes people who were far from him, living as they pleased (actually his enemies), and he turns them into family, treating them as family. Then he begins to show us how to behave in the family, to do the kinds of things he likes. Because we belong to God, he doesn't let us do whatever we feel like or live any way we want. He wants us to live in the way called "holy" – a way that shows we belong to him and that demonstrates what he is like.

God explained this to his people after he had rescued them from slavery, when they were still meeting with him at Mount Sinai: "I, the Lord, am the one who brought you up from the land of Egypt, that I might be your God. Therefore, you must be holy because I am holy" (Leviticus 11:45). Jesus talked about the same reality this way: "If you love me, obey my commandments" (John 14:15). We need to learn to live in the family.

Our relationship with God is both secure and demanding, which can be a problem for us. It is hard to hold on to both these realities at the same time and with equal strength. It is common to talk a lot about what God expects of us and forget that we are safe and secure in him. Preachers can talk about God's rules, but say little about his gifts. Or we talk about being secure and begin to think that we don't need to do anything else to please him. Maybe God likes forgiving us when we hurt him again and again? But in the covenant, "secure" and "demanding" go together. We belong to him.

Full of purpose

Our covenant relationship with God is also full of purpose. Part of our purpose in God's family is to bring him honour and glory.

Our son is studying overseas and doing very well. As his father and mother, we are very proud and we tell people about him. He came to visit us. Together we went back to the village where we lived when he was born. It was a celebration for everybody! People said, "This is our son. His victory is ours too!"

Jesus restores us from shameful outsiders to family members.

The same is true for us as God's own children. Because we are his very own, we either give him honour, or we shame him. God created the world, including humans, to bring him glory and honour. However, our sin damaged God's creation and brought us shame and dishonour. God wants us to remove our shame. He invites us to join him in restoring creation and bringing him glory.

So for the honour of his name, God leads his sinning people to repentance (Ezekiel 20:9, 14, 22) and treats us mercifully (Ezekiel 20:44). He does this so that we and the nations of the whole world will know his glory through us: "I will show how holy my great name is . . . When I reveal my holiness *through you* before their very eyes, says the Sovereign Lord, then the nations will know that I am the Lord" (Ezekiel 36:23, my emphasis).

This seems incredible. We are so broken and full of shame. In fact, we are as good as dead. But then we hear about a great vision: God by his Spirit brings very dry bones back to full life (Ezekiel 37)! Death does not defeat his purpose.

This is what God does in Jesus. Remember, making a covenant meant making an oath, saying originally, "May I die if I fail in my commitment to you. May I be cursed." God didn't fail, but his people did, and his people still do today. Our failure puts us under the curse of death. We deserve to be chopped up in little pieces like those animals in the covenant ceremony.

But God, who had already humbled himself to become like a human being and make a covenant, humbled himself again. In Jesus, he took the place of his failing, cursed people. Jesus died on the cross. He took on himself the shame of a criminal's death and the covenant penalty. Jesus rose again, breaking the power of sin, shame, and death. He began God's new creation, sending his new life out to every people in every corner of the world. Jesus restores us from shameful outsiders to family members. Now, we have the responsibility to live in the power of his name and proclaim it to others.

When God makes covenants in the Bible, he creates a people who belong to him in a relationship that is:

- **exclusive** – no room for any other god,
- **secure** – guaranteed by his own life,
- **demanding** – we must show that we belong to him, and
- **full of purpose** – with him we declare his glory throughout his world.

God used a well-known ancient custom in a brand-new way to communicate a whole new reality: in Jesus, he is making us a people for himself, his very own family.

It's hard to absorb all this. Living as who we really are in the covenant is even harder – and better. God has given us a human drama to help illustrate, and that is the theme we will follow in the next chapter.

SIX

WHAT A COVENANT LOOKS LIKE

I remember our wedding day. I stood at the front of the church, trembling, waiting. Then my bride came down the aisle, shimmering. She was glorious, and for me!

Every culture celebrates weddings. Here in Mozambique, there is a tradition that brides should not smile. (My bride smiled, wonderfully.) Someone explained that it shouldn't look like the bride is happy to be leaving her family. Nonetheless, even the bride who does not smile is very, very happy. And everyone else is free to show it. Usually there are several hours of waiting between the wedding ceremony and the feast. Groups of young people fill the time, clapping, singing, dancing in circles, and raising huge clouds of dust, each trying to outdo the others in their joy.

Astonishingly, our joy at weddings reflects a deeper, greater joy. Our marriages are built on a pattern from God himself. Did you know that the Bible describes the relationship between God and his people as a marriage? It may sound strange, and it is very different from our marriages, but that is what the Bible says. Throughout the Old Testament and the New, God is pictured as married to his people by covenant. That beautiful phrase, "You will be my people, and I will be your God", is an echo of the language of wedding ceremonies in the ancient world. It is an official declaration that now there is a covenant. An intimate relationship, each belonging to the other, has been created. There is honour, there is favour.

God's marriage

The Old Testament speaks often of the adultery and unfaithfulness of God's people. To pray to and serve other gods is to "lust after" them (Exodus 34:15), to "commit adultery against me" (Exodus 34:16), to "be unfaithful" (Leviticus 17:7), to "defile" oneself (Numbers 25:1), and to "become a prostitute" (Isaiah 1:21). The idea is that by making a covenant with his people, God has married them. He is the husband. The people are the wife.

Dozens of times the prophets talked this way. They spoke of "daughter Zion", "girl Zion", "mother Jerusalem", or "mother Israel". Sometimes this feminine figure was like an unmarried young woman; other times she was called a widow or divorced. She was the people of God being spoken of as his bride or wife. When she prayed or offered sacrifices or did some other ceremony to honour and serve some other "god" or spirit power, she was going for help to another man, not to her husband.

Idolatry is giving to another god or another person or thing the central place in our life and heart. Instead of depending on her husband, the wife was depending on someone else. It was like committing a sexual act with another man instead of the husband with whom she had made a covenant, the man she married. Only one person deserves the respect, attention, love, closeness, and trust of a husband. Allowing someone else into that place is a terrible offense.

We see this starkly in the case of the prophet Hosea, his wife Gomer, and their children. God told Hosea to marry a woman who was involved with other men. Hosea had to give his children names that meant "Not loved" and "Not my people" (Hosea 1:2-9). This was so that both the prophet and those around him would know and understand the hurt that was in God's heart. When the nation had left Egypt, God had married his bride, the people Israel (Hosea 2:1-23). He had cared for her tenderly. But as time went on, she looked to others for presents, to other lords, other husbands (in Hebrew, *lord* and *husband* can be the same word).

Time after time, God said things such as, *Let's sit down and talk through our problems. Tell me, haven't I been a good husband to you? How have I let you down?* Finally, angry, he said there would be a separation. He would take away all the good things he has been giving her. But divorce was no solution. He would win his wife's love back again. The marriage would be renewed.

Then in the next chapter (Hosea 3), the prophet had to do the same thing as God would do for Israel. He went after his wife, who had abandoned their home. He paid again to free her after she had become a slave through debts. He renewed love, not counting the pain, the offense, the humiliation, the sin. It was hard, very hard, to do this thing that God had called Hosea to endure. But the pattern was not just for Hosea. First, it was for God himself.

Jesus lived out and completed the story God was telling through Hosea. Jesus himself is the husband of his people, his bride (2 Corinthians 11:2). Jesus called himself "the bridegroom" (Matthew 9:15; Mark 2:19-20; Luke 5:34-35). God's people, Israel, his wife, had broken the covenant. They had not been faithful to him. It seemed like the covenant was at an end, that the marriage was broken forever.

But God would not give up, whatever it cost. In Jesus, he came himself into our world. On the cross, he took our shame and our guilt. He paid a great price for us. He paid for us with his very blood.

God longs to renew his people and his marriage to them. Paul speaks of a "great mystery" (Ephesians 5:32, and earlier): Christ and his people joined as one body, with Christ the husband who cares for and perfects his bride, the church. The book of Revelation, in closing the whole Bible, tells of a great wedding day when Jesus and his people will live together forever at last (Revelation 21:2-3). Finally, Christ will have a beautiful, holy, joyous bride.

One man from a church in town had a baking business with a partner from back in the village. Both of them did the work, but one week one of them would buy the flour, the firewood, and the yeast and then keep all the money from bread sales. The next week the other partner would have his turn.

After six months, the man from church was barely covering expenses, while his partner was consistently making a good profit. Asked about it, the partner said: "I had the spirits of the ancestors bless my business before we started! Didn't you?"

The believer asked me, "I've been praying to God. Should I do the ceremonies, too?"

It can seem so sensible to go to whatever power will get us what we want and need. Sometimes that might even be in church. Sometimes a diviner or "doctor" will seem like a better solution. But that is not at all how God sees it. We are married to him! When we look to other spirit powers for help, we are like a wife who sells herself to other men because she thinks her husband is not bringing home enough money. So, I told the Christian baker not to seek help from the ancestors but to trust God alone.

> God's pattern for marriage is so different from what we see around us that it is hard to take seriously.

I have seen floor-to-ceiling posters with pictures of a prophet-healer-miracle worker. Of course, God does miracles. And he uses people. But I wonder if we do not sometimes look so much at the "man of God" we can see with our eyes that we forget who our true Husband is.

I once spoke to a group of university students. A young woman came up afterwards and told me that the thing she had noticed was nothing I had said. It was the way my wife looked at me during the talk! "When I am married," she said, "I want to look at my husband with that kind of love and respect." How much more so should we look to our heavenly Husband!

The other side of our marriage to God is that he honours us. He shares his status and glory with us. And we have access to him like no one else has. When my wife and I are standing in a group and she sees an ant crawling on my neck, she can take it off. But nobody else should. She is my wife, and a wife has privileges.

In Jesus, we have privileges with God. We are highly favoured.

Our marriages

Pastor Mulema had paid his fare and was riding with 30 other people on the open back of a small truck. People were talking about AIDS. The pastor said, "AIDS can be stopped. If one man and one woman are faithful to each other for their whole lives, they won't get it."

People shouted back, "That's crazy! No one could ever live that way! Where did you ever get such an idea?"

Of course, he got it from the Bible. God's pattern for marriage is so different from what we see around us that it is hard to take seriously. Yet God himself takes it so seriously that he lives it. And he wants us to do the same.

You probably know a bad marriage or two. You have seen broken marriages and confused arrangements that were not-quite-marriages. In fact, those could be the only unions you have known. Good ones are hard to find (and they take hard work to keep up).

Understandably, we tend to look at the problems all around us and never notice God's pattern. Tradition tells one set of things about marriage. The modern world tells us many more. In some countries of the world, wealthy people actually have their lawyers prepare a prenuptial agreement for them to sign before the wedding, spelling out who will get what money and property if the marriage breaks up. It is as if they are already looking forward to a divorce!

None of this is even close to what God wants for us. In our world, social problems swirl around marriage. Wives are beaten. HIV/AIDS multiplies. Children are abandoned. Divorces seem normal. People get hurt. Few things cause more tears or deeper anguish.

Yet God says: Do not give up. I don't. I have given you a pattern in everyday life that comes from me and points to me. Live it!

It is easy to forget that marriage is a good thing. But in the Bible, there is no question about this. Marriage is good. God gave it to us. We see it already in Genesis 1 when God created humanity, male and female, in his image and everything was very good. Even more clearly, in Genesis 2, God brought Eve to Adam, joined them, making them one flesh, naked without shame because they were giving themselves to each other without keeping anything back.

Sin came afterward, in chapter 3, wrecking many things. But marriage is still a good gift from God.

Two of the Wisdom books in the Old Testament show us the beauty of marriage. In the book of Proverbs, parents give advice to their youthful sons. Of course, a lot of good advice for everybody appears in the book, but there is a special focus on young men. Wisdom, based on fearing the Lord, is portrayed as a lady worth seeking out. Folly is like another kind of woman, an adulteress. Though she lures you, stay away. Then, at the end of the book, in Proverbs 31, what blessing is there for a wise young man? A wonderful wife who brings him honour.

In the book Song of Songs, husband and wife declare their desire for each other in lush poetry that echoes the Garden of Eden. In a feast of words, they celebrate their intimacy, the joy of love and trust and giving themselves to each other. A chorus of friends sings along with them, because marriage is good.

In the New Testament, Jesus' first miracle in the Gospel of John was at a wedding celebration in Cana of Galilee (John 2:1-11).

We need lots of counsel and, perhaps, dozens of other books besides this one to try to recover marriages that aren't good and to strengthen marriages that are weak. We need brothers and sisters, fathers and mothers in the family of God to tell us and teach us and show us and help us. We need a strong love from God that can't be found in our own hearts where we sometimes scrape right down to the bottom and find only bitterness and resentment!

But marriage is worth it. Marriage matters. And for us, the people who belong to God, we have all we need from him and in him, our Lord, our Husband.

But we do need to be careful about these things. We must not think that only married people are close to God, or that only married people have maturity and spiritual understanding. The same apostle, Paul, who praised marriage, was a single man who argued that there are many advantages to not marrying when we serve God in this difficult world (1 Corinthians 7:25-35). God has put marriage near each one of us so we can understand better his relationship with us. This doesn't mean, however, that everyone should be married.

Yes, God loves. But, more than that, God is love. Loving is not just something he does; it is part of who he is inside.

There is another danger when we hear that God and Jesus are like a husband to us. Some husbands will begin yelling, "Do you hear that, wife? I am like Christ. I am like God. I am in charge around here!" Other husbands won't shout it, but they will think it.

The truth is that a husband does have authority and responsibility. But power can get misused. In our world, powerful people often abuse and exploit weaker people. We see this so much that we can think it's normal. But that is not how God makes us to be.

One man from South Sudan told me he had shocked the whole village. His wife was sick, and he took the family laundry down to the river and washed it himself, then hung it out. No man had ever done that!

But our pattern comes from God's marriage to his people. The husband serves and sacrifices in love. The Bible does not authorize abuse or dictatorship. Besides, God gives a wife wisdom and understanding. A husband loses when he doesn't listen and learn from his wife.

In Ephesians 5, what does it say about the husband and his responsibility to be like Christ? He has to love his wife and sacrifice himself for her, seeking what is best for her, meeting her needs, caring for her at all costs. That is what it means to say "love".

It is written, "God is love" (1 John 4:8, 16). Pay attention. It doesn't just say in these verses that God loves us, that he rescues sinners. It says something bigger. Yes, God loves. But, more than that, God *is* love. Loving is not just something he does; it is part of who he is inside. Even before creating us, God is love.

The Trinity is implied: Father, Son, and Holy Spirit, one and only God, loving each other with a love so perfect and so abundant that it overflows into creating a universe and filling a world with people to be loved. It is a love so strong and so lasting that it won't let sin win. It is a love that makes covenant, resting us and challenging us. It is a love that wants to be loved back.

God created marriage so that in our day-to-day lives we could demonstrate covenant and declare the character of the God who makes covenant. In the Bible, love is not just a passing desire. It is much stronger. It makes and keeps covenant. And this is how our marriages are meant to be. They should live out this kind of love and commitment.

In this book, we've already followed a phrase: "You will be my people, and I will be your God." We've looked closely at a powerful word: *covenant.* Just now we have seen a live-action drama: marriage.

But there is a big problem: if we are so highly favoured by God in his covenant, why do we suffer? That is where we will go in the next chapter.

SEVEN

DOES THE COVENANT PREVENT SUFFERING?

The Mumaahi evangelism team was on the way. It had been raining hard for three days. Thick red mud stuck to the Land Rover's wheels. It could barely make it up the hill. Going down the other side was worse. The car skidded sideways and nearly ended up in the bush. The bridge at the bottom of the hill was under water. Then a tyre went flat. One brother said to the others, "The Devil is against our journey."

A faithful mother, Maria, lost one child to malaria. The other lived, but had convulsions again and again. Her husband had gone away. She tested positive for HIV. She was supposed to eat proteins and fruit, but could barely manage dried manioc and boiled leaves. She said in her heart, "God doesn't care for me."

I remember standing on the fresh earth of a newly-dug grave, as we buried our seven-year-old daughter, also lost to malaria. I looked into the faces of the women and men from the church standing there with us, together in pain. Almost every one of them had lost a daughter or a son during years of war, hardship, and poverty. It was a hard comfort, realizing that our pain was shared.

But there was also a deep doubt. How is it that the people of God can suffer like this? What had the little one done to deserve it? My family and I had given ourselves to the Lord to serve him in a civil war in one of the poorest places on earth. Instead of running from dangers, we had stayed committed. But where were the protection and power of God? We prayed, "God, weren't you supposed to take care of us? Where were you? We went out on a limb risking ourselves for you. Why did you chop off the branch that held us up?"

Years later, the church in our part of the country sent one of its first Mozambican missionaries to another province, to plant churches in an area both Muslim and pagan. He was one of the few leaders with Bible school training. He committed himself, with his wife and three daughters, to live among people he didn't know, with a language and customs that were new to him. After just two years, he got sick, with bleeding that would not stop. He had hospital treatment for months. He even had some time in the central hospital in the capital city. But none of it was enough. He died, leaving a family and church in grief.

Is this the way God takes care of his dear servants?

A good God, an ugly world

Each one of us has our own stories to add to these: people who belong to God, are trying to do the right thing, and have terrible things happen to them. If we are the covenant people of God, rich in privileges and promises, how come we have such a hard time? If the favour of God is part of our lives, how can we face so many defeats?

> We have not been raised above to a higher plane of guaranteed prosperity, abundance, and good health.

All suffering in this world challenges us and challenges our faith. But even worse for our faith is when we suffer as believers. We are his people, he is our God! How can he let all these things happen to us?

I am not going to pretend to deal here with the whole problem of suffering. It is too big. We have cried together before, and we will cry together again. But I do want to share with you some of what the Lord has woven into our lives as we have grieved over our daughter, as we have grieved over other hurts, as we have grieved with those around us.

When our daughter died, we had been working through the

Psalms with the Elomwe translation team. The hard edges and sharp emotions of these psalms worked their way into our grief, shaping us and stiffening us. The two surprises we talked about at the beginning of this book have both become more real for us: first, that we already have the favour of God; second, that this favour we already have in Jesus is better than we think and better than we ask for. It's that second surprise that is the heart of this chapter.

Right near the start, Psalms reminds us of reality:

> *Why are the nations so angry? Why do they waste their*
> *time with futile plans? The kings of the earth prepare*
> *for battle; the rulers plot together against the Lord*
> *and against his anointed one.*
> PSALM 2:1-2

This world has big problems. Things are not right. The world is full of noise and confusion, violence and destruction, disease and poverty. Both peoples and leaders are involved. And we could say that the anger and confusion is right there, way down in our individual hearts as well. There are times when I know I am supposed to pray, when I actually want to pray, and yet I think of a thousand other things – resentments and hurts – and then don't pray.

The psalm explains that what is wrong with this world, and with us, is that mankind doesn't want God to be in charge. This whole world system is in loud revolt against God and his chosen ruler, his Messiah, his Christ. So we shouldn't expect it to be full of peace, prosperity, and contentment. In fact, the apostle Paul says, the whole of creation is groaning right now, waiting for release (Romans 8:22). We cannot insist, as Christians, that we are immune to these conditions. We have not been raised above to a higher plane of guaranteed prosperity, abundance, and good health. Some of the "groaning" comes from us!

But God is not threatened by all the noise. Up in heaven, he rules. Down on earth, too, he rules, through the king he has chosen, the Christ. Psalm 2:4 says that God actually laughs at the noise.

I once came face to face with a lion, a male lion with a big mane. He roared, and a lion's roar will take you places you have never been. It is so deep it will reach inside and grab your bones and rattle them. But actually, I wasn't scared. I *was* physically shaken, and I didn't laugh, but I wasn't really scared. It's not because I'm such a fool, either. It's because the lion was in the zoo in Lisbon, Portugal, and there were some nice, thick steel bars keeping him from me.

God is in charge, his Christ is in charge, and he knows it. He is not scared at all. It's just the world that is confused. And it's the world and its people who ought to be scared. The psalm says to smarten up, submit, and serve him. In a messed-up world, there is joy when we take refuge in him.

This psalm takes evil seriously, but takes God and his control even more seriously. I think a drunken teenager at a checkpoint pointing an AK-47 is even more scary than a lion. But Psalm 2 tells me that even there, Jesus rules. We belong to him, by covenant. It's no surprise when the world that hates him hurts us (John 15:18). And he is taking care of us, when the gun does not fire, but also when it does.

How long, O Lord?

However, there are so many times when things don't feel that way.

> *O Lord, how long will you forget me? For ever?*
> *How long will you look the other way?*
> PSALM 13:1

In this passage, a believer is praying. And complaining. His situation has been bad and still is bad. Enemies are out to kill him, and they are very close to succeeding (13:2-3). There is "sorrow in [his] heart every day." The awful shame of defeat is staring him in the face. Four different times he asks the accusing question: "How long?" In his crisis, God isn't doing anything. Time is passing. He has already asked for God's help. And there is no solution in sight.

Have you ever heard anyone pray like that? In the churches I am used to, people might think it disrespectful to talk to God that way. When you talk to the big boss in that tone, he is more likely to get angry than he is to help. It will just make things worse. Better to shut up about our doubts. I think we often think this way. And sometimes we dress it up as theology. We think we need to always have a loud, positive, "of-course-God-will-give-it-to-me" faith. If we haven't yet got what we want, we must not have been loud and positive enough.

But that is not how this psalm works. There is no shutting up about doubts. There are loud calls to God. God is blamed for looking the other way, for abandoning the believer. And sometimes that is how I need to pray. I need to tell God how desolate everything seems, how disappointed and hurt I am.

A couple came to me in the big city. They were educated. They both had good jobs. They had been married five years. But they had no children. Their families were murmuring, blaming. They needed to pray: "Lord, how long?"

Pay attention, though: this believer in Psalm 13 is talking to the Lord. Right in the first line, he brings his problem directly to God. He doesn't say to himself, *Since God let me down, since I can't see a solution, I'm going to go find some other way.* He doesn't go to other people (or other powers) and complain about how the Lord is failing him. Frustrated, he takes his problem to the boss himself. He is hurting, but the relationship is still exclusive.

In fact, the complaint assumes that God has made promises, guarantees, and commitments to his people. I can't ask "How long?" of someone who never said he would help me. If a friend and I have agreed to do something together on a certain day and he doesn't come, I might text him: "How long until you get here?" I would never do that if we hadn't made a plan together in the first place. It is because of his promise to me that I am disappointed and wondering.

In this psalm, the one who speaks knows that the Lord has taken on himself the responsibility of caring for his people. He knows that covenant obligations bind God as well as his people. He has a right to complain. And it is worth complaining because God will answer.

The last two verses of Psalm 13 seem to come from a completely different psalm. They start with "But I". His enemies are still out there, doing what they do. God's help is very late. But the psalmist has made up his mind about what he is going to do: "trust in your unfailing love"! He is so sure of God's covenant goodness that he can already declare his confidence and begin to celebrate: "I will rejoice because you have rescued me." It is too soon for the external situation to have changed; yet after his complaining prayer, the way is opened to praise and singing and thanks.

Of course, our wonderful freedom to complain is not a freedom to command. We don't give God orders. He is still in charge.

We saw in the last chapter that God's covenant relationship with his people is a marriage. I can imagine a wife complaining to her husband, "How long?" There is a problem with their house, a door that doesn't close properly. She doesn't criticize her husband to all her neighbours. Certainly she doesn't look for some other man to come fix the door. But privately she asks him, "How long are you going to leave things this way?"

She knows he will deal with the problem. She knows she is loved. She isn't nervous about bringing up what is bothering her. When her good husband says, "Okay, I'll fix it," she starts smiling. In Elomwe we would say, "Her heart sits down." Even though the door still doesn't close like it should, she trusts him. The problem is being taken care of. Her husband is dealing with it.

For the couple without children, just praying "How long?" gave them courage. They were confident to complain. And for our family, the freedom to hurt and to tell God, again and again, "It hurts! It still hurts! How long?" is a huge comfort. We can sing that God is good.

Even Jesus suffered

Of course, our wonderful freedom to complain is not a freedom to command. We don't give God orders. He is still in charge. He understands both the beginning of things and their end in ways we do not. Many Lomwe people have a little formula near the end of their prayers: "Lord, I'm not telling you what to do, I'm just asking." It is a good habit.

It is important to realize something else. It is not just that we hurt. Jesus, our covenant Lord, has suffered too, with us and for us. Here is the beginning of another psalm:

My God, my God, why have you abandoned me?
PSALM 22:1

These words are the cry of God's faithful servant David, left alone and suffering. He begs for relief and sees only evil (22:2). He realizes that God is holy and has always been faithful, but he feels deep shame. He doesn't even count as a human being. Lots of people know he has been trusting in God, and it's all for nothing (22:6-8).

Nonetheless he calls out, "My God, my God!" He knows God belongs to him and that he belongs to God. Even in pain, he is declaring his trust. He uses the covenant language of "my God" when it doesn't look like God is keeping the covenant. He knows he has belonged to God since he was born (22:9-10). Now, in crisis, there is no other solution (22:11-21). His enemies are bulls, they are lions, they are dogs. They have pierced him through, hands and feet (22:16); they have grabbed away his clothing (22:18). And he doesn't stop pleading to God: "Save me . . . spare my precious life!" (22:20-21). This is amazing: covenant gives him the right to complain and to trust at the same time.

From then on, it seems like a whole different psalm. The servant, so abandoned, praises God along with many of the Lord's people (22:22-25). The afflicted and miserable are satisfied (22:26). People from the far ends of the earth submit to God's rule (22:27-29). There are wonderful things to declare to future generations: "They will hear about everything he has done" (22:31).

What has God done? He acted; he did what was right. He intervened, fulfilling his covenant commitments. He didn't walk away from the one who belonged to him. The faithful servant in the psalm declares that God answered his cry for help (22:24), though he doesn't say how. But what God did was right. It was what he ought to have done. He had an obligation. He had to act.

On the cross, Jesus called out, "My God, my God, why have you abandoned me?" (Matthew 27:46). He was the servant of servants, the most faithful of the faithful. Carrying the weight of all our sin, our guilt and failure and shame, all the evil of a world that has lost direction, rebelling against its Creator, God handed him over to punishment. Our punishment. Jesus died in agony.

But the covenant God did what is right and made things right. He demonstrated his justice; he vindicated his own. He raised Jesus from the dead. In Jesus, he launched the life of the new creation. And Jesus, in his cry of pain, declared his faith that this is what God, the God of covenant, is like.

Paul, in prison, wrote about being glad he was "participating in the sufferings of Christ" (Colossians 1:24). I have learned to be glad that Jesus has participated in our sufferings.

A few years after our daughter died, the man I thought was my closest friend in Mozambique conspired to expel us from our house, multiplying lies. The first hurt made the second one worse. And it is sweet to know that my Jesus knows exactly what it feels like to be betrayed. It is harder to be glad about participating in Christ's sufferings. But *covenant* means we belong to him, and a world that hates him is going to hate us too. That man's betrayal wasn't just against me. He was rejecting Jesus, and I can be honoured to share in Jesus' shame.

Suffering that is justified

I have been talking about pain and suffering that we don't seem to deserve. But that is not the only kind we see in the Psalms.

> *Oh, what joy for those whose disobedience is forgiven,*
> *whose sin is put out of sight!*
> PSALM 32:1

David begins with joy, the delight of being forgiven (32:1-2). Then he tells some of his own story. There was a time of terrible pain, when his body had no strength, when groaning didn't stop. That was when he was trying to hide the sin he had committed (32:3-4). But when he told everything to the Lord, confessing his sin, there was forgiveness. There was relief (32:5). Close to the Lord there was such deep safety that even the raging ocean was no threat (32:6-7).

With safety came a promise. God promised David that he would keep watching him, that he would be looking at him to guide and counsel him every day (32:8). But the promise came with a warning: "Do not be like a senseless horse or mule" (32:9). Horses and mules have a metal bit tied into their mouths to steer them. They turn to one side or the other when they feel pressure in their mouths, as their rider pulls on the piece of metal. Without pain, they don't obey.

God's advice is: learn to listen to what I say before it hurts. I will hurt you if I have to, to get your attention, but it's so much better when I don't have to. People who are stuck doing wrong will suffer for it, but those who trust in the Lord have a right to covenant love and care (32:10). The psalm began with one person's praise; it ends with the joyous worship of all God's people (32:11).

From beginning to end, this psalm assumes covenant. Sure, there is a general principle that someone who does good should expect good and someone who does evil should expect evil. But in the covenant, there is commitment. There are mutual obligations. God does not walk away from those who fail. He works so that the covenant can be restored.

David tells us in the psalm that he had done wrong, and he was trying to hide it. So God made him miserable. He put pain into David's life to get his attention.

God wants what is best for us more than we want it ourselves. He will do whatever it takes to get us what we need. Sometimes that means hurting us. It also means that with repentance, the sinner is welcomed, safe, and close to God. God's tender advice is that it is so much better to do what he says in the first place, to learn from him without it having to hurt. There is an ongoing relationship of joy as a believer grows and walks with God. And God is committed to growing us.

In the case of our daughter's death, my wife and I don't see a connection to a personal sin, though of course we have wondered a thousand times about things we could have done differently. But in the case of the betrayal, I have come to see that over the preceding years, this man had lied about and betrayed other people. I believed his lies and went along with his betrayals, supporting my friend. This made me complicit in hurting a lot of other innocent people. It is a guilt and shame I have had to repent of. And forgiveness is sweet, very sweet.

We have no explanation. And, still, covenant gives us the confidence to demand that God act for us, because his love is real.

God has also used both of these hurts, the death and the

betrayal, to grow us. We are more sensitive to other people and their hurts. We are less arrogant and self-assured, less confident in our own cleverness and more confident in Jesus.

May we accuse God?

Other psalms make it clear that our sin and its consequences are only part of the story. Psalm 44 begins this way:

O God, we have heard it with our own ears – our ancestors have told us of all you did in their day, in days long ago.
PSALM 44:1

This is also a complaining prayer, like Psalms 13 and 22. This time the focus isn't on one person, but on the whole of God's people.

History is clear: Ever since the times of our ancestors, God has been faithful to his covenant with his people. They were given a whole land to live in, and it wasn't because of their own ability or military power. It was the presence and power of the Lord himself that helped them: "It was your right hand and strong arm and the blinding light from your face that helped them, for you loved them" (44:3).

This hasn't been forgotten, either. Here and now, a warrior declares, "I do not trust in my bow; I do not count on my sword to save me. You are the one who gives us victory over our enemies" (44:6-7). The people praise God and give glory to him.

But something terrible has happened, the psalmist goes on to say. This time we didn't win. Our enemies trampled all over us. We were slaughtered like animals. We ran. Others have been captured and sold as slaves. And it's all God's fault! *You* didn't lead the army like you should have (44:9). *You* tossed us aside! *You* have butchered us! *You* sold us! (44:9-14). The people are speaking these things to God, piling on accusations.

The problem is not just the awful shame of defeat. It is that we didn't deserve it, they say. In the covenant, we know we can't ignore God and get away with it. We expect that disobedience will be punished because that is what our loving Father promised (see Psalm 32). But this time, "we have not forgotten you. We have not violated your covenant" (44:17). We are innocent! We know we can't get away with pretending, either. You know our heart secrets (44:20-21).

The problem here is a covenant problem: the covenant God, always faithful, has seemingly failed his covenant people. How could this happen?

And this psalm never gives an answer. God doesn't give an explanation. What comes next is a plea. It seems like God is asleep, letting things get worse and worse. But the plea comes as a string of commands, telling God what to do: Wake up! Get up! Help us! Ransom us! (44:23-26). The last word of the psalm is translated "unfailing love". It is specially a word for covenant relationship. We see what looks like God's failure. We have no explanation. And, still, covenant gives us the confidence to demand that he act for us, because his love is real.

In the years after our daughter died, our other two children also got malaria. Our son, the youngest, got it again and again. We felt like shrieking, "Lord, this is too much!" And we begged for help. It did not feel like victory at all.

Victory is wonderful. God promises it. But it is easy to promise a false victory. Alongside the road, the day before yesterday, was a white sheet hung up on a bamboo frame, painted to make a sign. "The famous Tanzanian doctor Makisi! Cures for AIDS, for infertility! Protection from enemies!" All, of course, for a price, to be negotiated. And there are churches that promise Christians victory and healing in almost the same way, also for a price. They have no place for the mysteries of hurt and defeat along the way to final victory. They have no place for what the Lord told the apostle Paul who had prayed three times for healing: Each time he said, "My grace is all you need. My power works best in weakness"

(2 Corinthians 12:9). Jesus is the victor in his resurrection and finally at his return. In between we share in his victory and in defeats we cannot explain.

Time out to ponder

There is one other psalm we need to consider. It warns us that suffering and injustice can twist our thinking. It begins like this:

> *Truly God is good to Israel, to those whose hearts are pure.*
> *But as for me, I almost lost my footing. My feet were slipping,*
> *and I was almost gone. For I envied the proud when I saw*
> *them prosper despite their wickedness.*
> PSALM 73:1-3

This psalmist, called Asaph, is clear: God is good to his people. But there was a problem. Asaph saw bad guys doing very well indeed, and it nearly ruined him.

More details follow: the bad guys "seem to live such painless lives" (73:4). They don't have the problems everybody else does (73:5). They do whatever they feel like, and everybody goes along with them (73:8-10). They even scoff at God, then watch their money multiply (73:11-12).

A young lady in secondary school saw her friends get good marks by sleeping with the teachers. By not sleeping with the teachers, she would get bad marks, however much she studied. What should she do? "Fix" her problem by doing evil?

In the same way, Asaph was discouraged, too. "Did I keep my heart pure for nothing?" (73:13). Doing the right thing only got him trouble (73:14).

But then he went into God's presence to reflect (73:17). There he realized that the wicked are not doing as well as it seems. Their bustling wealth is like the agitated activity of a dream. You wake up and it all fades away (73:19-20). He realized he hadn't been thinking straight, more like a beast than a man (73:22).

So he turned his thoughts to his relationship with the Lord: "I still belong to you; you hold my right hand" (73:23). Neither in earth nor in heaven is anyone more precious. His body may fall apart, but with God his heart is strong (73:25-26). There is something that matters more than things going well or going badly: being close to God or far away from him (73:27-28).

Covenant commitment, the love that comes when we belong to God, gave Asaph a secure place to complain, to reflect, and finally to understand reality in a new way. "Good" and "bad" got new definitions. It was not simply prosperity versus poverty, health versus sickness. At the deepest level, good is being close to God, bad is being far away from him.

In Romans 8:28, Paul explains that God works through all the moments and events of our lives for our good. The good he is talking about fits his plan and purpose for us. Then in the next verse, Paul explains that God is transforming us to make us conform to Jesus, so we will have a character like that of Jesus.

This is perhaps the hardest thing for us. We are sure we know what is good: prospering in business, getting good marks in school, being healthy. And we are right; those and many more things are all good things. But are they the best things? How important to us is being close to God?

> Instead of analysing what Satan is doing, they hand everything over to God.

A small child thinks she knows what is good. She wants to play with the sharp, shiny knife that her mother uses so much. It is in fact a good, useful, and beautiful thing. But her mother, in love, will take the knife away, say no, and distract the child with something else, because she knows what the child doesn't know. What the child wants can hurt her very much. There are times when our Father doesn't please us and we end up crying. But he has taken something away from us to give us something better, to help us to grow.

This is very hard for me. For years, up until that friend betrayed me, we had worked very closely with just one denomination. A good thing! And then we lost some of that connection and were forced to work with many more churches. Now I can see that the finished Elomwe Bible would have been seen as belonging to only the one denomination, whereas now it is seen as being for all the churches.

But there is something bigger than the strategic change that is clear to me now. For a long time in the middle, things didn't make sense. I felt ashamed and confused. And that was good because I was forced to ask God again and again, "What do *you* want?" I was forced to depend more on him and less on my reputation.

We need so many things in this world, and we like so many things – good gifts from God. Sadly, we can focus on these things so much that we lose out on the deeper satisfaction of knowing God himself in Christ and of finding in him our joy, our strength, and our best.

What about Satan?

I have been bringing you along the path God has used in our grief, sharing themes from the psalms that have been especially good for my wife and me when we have faced great suffering. By now, you might wonder about something else: Where is the Devil in all this? Doesn't Satan prowl around like a roaring lion, eager to eat us up (1 Peter 5:8)? Doesn't the apostle John talk about Satan manipulating Judas to betray Jesus (John 13:27)?

We know Satan is real. We know he attacks us. But none of these psalms even mentions Satan. The Devil gets no space. What is going on?

The Psalms have lots to say about enemies, but very little to say about the Enemy. The book of Job, however, does talk about Satan. It was years after translating Psalms that we came to translate Job, and it was slow, painstaking work. The Hebrew of Job is very complicated. That gave me lots of time to reflect on what Job tells us about Satan.

Job was a good man and faithful to God. God himself said so. Job suffered terribly but couldn't see anything he had done wrong to cause it all. In fact, he could see only part of his own story. He argued with his friends for chapter after chapter. He appealed to God and complained about the unfairness of what was happening to him. But he didn't talk about Satan; still less did he talk to Satan.

On the other hand, we, the book's readers, are told in the first two chapters that there was a contest going on in the unseen world. The accuser, Satan, had gone to God and argued that Job obeyed God only because of the blessings he received. God disagreed. God allowed Satan to take away Job's blessings and to attack Job with terrible sufferings, but God carefully limited what Satan could do.

The Lord was the one in charge. And poor Job was never told any of this. Even at the very end of the book, when Job met directly with God, he was never told what we readers know.

Clearly, the Devil is active, but he has to get God's permission before attacking. He doesn't touch the Lord's people without authorization. That is why neither Job nor the psalmists pay much attention to Satan. They know all sorts of enemies are lurking out there, seen and unseen. But they run to the Lord for solutions. Instead of analysing what Satan is doing, they hand everything over to God.

And the big question behind all that happened to Job is something for us to ask ourselves: Are we in it just for the blessings? Or are we in it for God himself?

A church executive meeting went on until three o'clock in the morning. The problem was an older pastor who had been repeatedly accused of witchcraft. No one was actually suggesting that he be disciplined; instead the proposal was that he be required to retire because of his age, keeping up appearances all around.

I listened to the discussion, saying nothing. Finally, the chairman asked me point-blank for my opinion. I said there was no way such a man should continue in ministry. That decided the meeting.

And the accused man gave me a very intense look, saying, "Foster, you'll see!"

At four o'clock I crawled into our family tent. At six we all got up and started to get ready for a big, closing church service. But something was wrong with our four-year-old son's legs. They buckled. He couldn't walk. I thought he was tired and would get better.

Hours later, a doctor who was there examined him and diagnosed a viral infection spreading up from his feet that could kill him quickly. He needed advanced medical care available only out of the country – more than 12 hours' drive away. Amazingly, the Lord provided an airplane so that an hour after noon we were in the air and on the way.

No sooner had we got above the clouds than our son said, "Daddy, my legs are fine." Sure enough, at the sophisticated hospital that evening and the next day, there was no sickness to be found.

I must confess that my only prayer as we scrambled to cope with the crisis had been, "Help, Lord!" Others prayed at more length: "Lord, protect! Lord, provide! Lord, defend! Lord, heal!"

Were demonic powers active? I think so. Was there anyone besides the Lord to whom we could turn for rescue? No. Praise God that attack was over and done.

But grief is more complicated. Years after our younger daughter died, we celebrated her sister's wedding. In all our joy, we felt pain underneath as well. The sister who should have been there was not. And just as with Job, God has never explained why. Some parts of our own story don't make sense to us.

And that is okay, because holding on to God himself is the bigger thing. God is the one who understands the big story. We just have to look to him. The deeper satisfaction is knowing God himself in Christ, finding in him our joy, our strength, our best.

Through covenant, we know that he is our God and that we are his people. We have his help as we deal with suffering. Above all, we have Jesus.

EIGHT

TIED FOREVER TO JESUS

Belonging is vital. Literally. A tomato plant uprooted is already withering and dying. A person who has nobody also dies. That is obvious for a newborn baby abandoned in the rubbish pit. But it is also true for a vigorous young man who doesn't feel that he belongs. He starts to multiply violence, robbery, and murder – death swirls around him. For any of us after death, it is a double death if no one cares for our body and gives us a decent burial.

However, belonging is also complicated. After church one day a man told me he had fled to town with his family, leaving his home and business, because he was afraid his children would be attacked. He had lived there for 20 years and prospered. He even had a little store. He was from the same ethnic group and spoke the same language as the people there. He had even been born in the same district, though some 80 kilometres away.

But cholera had come through the area, and the rumour was that someone was poisoning water supplies. Locals accused the *anamarwa*, the "incomers" – residents not seen as truly "ours", people who didn't really belong – and that included him. Mobs formed, and the storekeeper was warned: "They are coming for you next!"

Belonging to Jesus is the most important thing of all. In Genesis, God gave Adam and Eve a mission: to rule the world demonstrating who God is, showing his image. In Christ, the Adam-Adam, the new representative of humanity, we have those privileges and that mission as well: to demonstrate what God is like by how we live and what we do in this world. God made a covenant with

Abraham so that the blessings of being God's people would come to all the peoples of the world. He wanted to deal with the problem of sin and of his ruined world. And he wouldn't let his people's failings ruin his plan.

The prophets spoke of a remnant, a few faithful ones among a vast majority of stubborn, rebellious people. Finally, the remnant was down to just one completely faithful, committed person, Jesus. And this one took the penalty for failure.

Now, in him, the covenant cannot fail. In him, new creation has begun. The resurrection body of Jesus is already part of the new creation. We have to belong to Jesus – even though it is complicated.

Jesus suffers with us and also for us; he destroys the power of sin and the Devil. Jesus brings the new covenant.

In Jesus

The Old Testament ends with a question unanswered: has God failed? The story is incomplete. God has guaranteed everything to his people, making an oath commitment that puts his life on the line. But the people are still doing terribly. Only some of them are back in the Promised Land, and they are a colony of a pagan empire. Worse, the new heart and new life of the renewed covenant are a long way off.

Then comes Jesus. God is fulfilling his promises after all! In Jesus, the covenant that is so old is made new, renewed, and transformed. By Jesus's death and resurrection we belong to God and God to us. The New Testament declares that Jesus answers the unanswered questions and takes doubts away. Jesus suffers with us and also for us; he destroys the power of sin and the Devil. Jesus brings the new covenant.

All through the apostle Paul's letters, he talks about being joined to Jesus in covenant. *In* him, *through* him, *belonging* to him, God's goodness comes to us. Being declared right in the presence of God is for those who put their trust in Jesus (Romans 3:22). Being bought back from slavery to sin and death is "through Christ Jesus"

(Romans 3:24). There is no "condemnation for those who belong to Christ Jesus" (Romans 8:1). At the end of that same chapter, God's love for us is "in Christ Jesus" (Romans 8:39). And these are just examples from Romans! In total, Paul uses this wording almost a hundred times. Read the letters and you will see it all over the place.

All the blessings, privileges, power and protection, all the forgiveness of sins, all our honour and hope of glory – everything that belongs to the people who belong to God – is ours in Jesus though covenant with him. The apostle Peter echoes the same language while saying goodbye at the end of his letter: "Peace be with all of you who are in Christ" (1 Peter 5:14). This is how we are spoken of. This is where we belong. If we are connected, we have everything. But if we are disconnected, we have nothing.

Another way of talking about the same reality is the phrase "body of Christ". The church, the people of God, is called the body of Christ in this world, so joined to him that it is actually part of him (Romans 12; 1 Corinthians 12; Ephesians 1:23; 4:4; Colossians 1:18). It is active in this world, acting through him. We are alive and fruitful in this world, because we belong to him.

But how do we belong? It is a miracle that God's Spirit performs as we repent and trust Jesus. This is what the New Testament tells us, focusing everything on Jesus. And it tells us that he has given us baptism and the Lord's Supper as powerful, public ways of enacting our covenant commitment to him. These are covenant signs that the Spirit uses to communicate and confirm heart reality.

As we trust Jesus, baptism and the Lord's Supper connect us to his reality. He gave us these two ceremonies. They are vivid dramas that we enact, powerful in the Spirit of God, to show us the truth of the new covenant. They are rich in all sorts of layers of meaning!

Baptism

I said earlier that belonging is complicated. One Sunday morning there was an announcement in church: A young man wanted to get married, but hadn't been baptized yet. The young woman's church required proof of baptism before there could be a wedding.

The young man thought that learning the catechism and passing the exam in order to get baptized would take too long. So he bribed the district secretary of the denomination to forge a pastor's signature on a baptism certificate! But it was all found out, when the pastor happened to see the forged document. And the wedding didn't happen.

Is that what baptism is? Church rules, bureaucracy, paperwork, and hoops to jump through in order to get married?

What if the young man had actually followed all the rules and gotten baptized properly? Suppose he was a church member in good standing with an honest letter of recommendation from his pastor back home. Would that make sure he belonged to Jesus?

When we speak about the people of God, lots of people think about a church they belong to or know of. This church has its structure and organization and rules. If you follow the expectations of the group, or at least look like you do, everything will be fine. One Lomwe church song declares that the rest of us are on a heavenly journey, but you, a sinner, are being left out and left behind. Maybe the women's group has a special uniform and a special meeting day. If you wear the uniform and come on the day, you will belong.

But will you belong to Jesus? Maybe, maybe not. It is easy for us to think our relationship with the visible group is the most important thing. Our relationship with God in Jesus, whom we cannot see – perhaps that happens automatically? Maybe it isn't all that important?

Sometimes we think that using the right slogans is all that we need. I have seen minibuses painted with "God only knows", a reference to Psalms, or even John 3:16. Maybe the owner is showing his deep trust in Jesus and thanks to God, but maybe he is thinking that the power of the religious words themselves will keep the vehicle from accidents. Is looking and sounding right enough?

That is not what we mean when we talk about a deep, even scary, commitment in Jesus to the God who makes covenant. It is by faith and the Spirit's miracle we enter this relationship that is so secure and so demanding.

The water of baptism is not just a washing. It is also a sign of judgement. The waters of the flood in the time of Noah brought punishment on the world of that time, but also lifted up the boat that saved Noah, his family, and the animals. The waters of the Red Sea destroyed Pharaoh's pursuing army and then made a barrier to protect the people of God. In the same way, baptism is a sign that we sinners deserve death under the judgement of God (see 1 Peter 3:20-21). Entering the water is a sign of death, and coming out of the water is a sign of resurrection (Romans 6:3-4).

When God made a covenant with Abraham, the sign was a cut on an intimate part of the male body. The cut speaks of punishment, of death deserved, the covenant curse for someone who breaks his commitment to belong to God. It was a sign of an oath sworn: "May I be cut off, if I don't keep the commitment I have made to God." In the new covenant, baptism is similar (Colossians 2:11-12), but with big differences, too. Our Jesus was baptized. Our Jesus died. Our Jesus rose again. This new covenant sign says our sins deserve the punishment of death, but Jesus took that punishment on himself for those who belong to him. It also speaks of God welcoming us into his life of new creation.

When Jesus was baptized by John in the Jordan River, something unusual happened. Other people went into the water and came out, declaring that their sin deserved God's judgement, deserved death. Each time God himself kept silence, accepting the declaration. When Jesus approached John for baptism, John said, "No! Not you!" But Jesus insisted, identifying himself with his sinful people (Matthew 3:14-15).

As he came out of the water, this time God spoke: "This is my dearly loved Son, who brings me great joy" (Matthew 3:17). God was saying, *No! This one doesn't deserve to die. I don't have a problem with this one.* He took away any doubt.

When Jesus died on the cross, God did the same thing. Jesus had been accused of being a liar, a false saviour. But God raised him from the dead, vindicating him, and giving him new creation life. God declared: *This one is in the right! He really is Saviour and Lord.*

When we are baptized, we enter into covenant with Jesus. We identify ourselves with him. He joined himself to our sin and took our punishment on the cross. Joined to him, his death took the place of God's punishment on us. His resurrection, as God vindicated him, is the guarantee of our resurrection, too. Joined to Jesus, we begin to have new creation life already in this world.

God takes baptism seriously. Baptism is a powerful declaration of real covenant allegiance. Even the spirits know it! An older woman was being baptized in the Molocué river. The pastor stood holding her ready to declare, "I baptize you". An elder stood in the water beside him. Suddenly the frail woman was filled with superhuman strength. She grabbed the pastor and forced him under the water. The elder and another man intervened and saved the pastor from drowning. Later, it was discovered that the woman had been part of a group that danced together in a ritual to summon the spirits some years before. When she became a believer, she stopped doing the dances. However, she had not renounced the dances and the spirit powers before the day of her baptism. These spirits took the sworn commitment of baptism seriously and protested with all their might. Do we take it seriously?

When Jesus was baptized, he was also marked out by the Holy Spirit. It is this same Spirit that acts in us so that the declarations of baptism are not empty symbols (let alone some church paperwork!), but realities we live by faith.

The Lord's Supper

The second new covenant sign Jesus gave us is his supper. (Different churches also use other names, like Communion or Eucharist.) It is also his feast.

Feasting is important in every culture. Many are welcomed, and good things are shared. Poverty and hardship make it all the more important. During Mozambique's civil war, our city had terrible shortages. It took us six weeks to buy our first bread. But the Coke factory still worked – if you had the empty bottles to refill. One man we knew was very popular because he owned three crates of empty bottles, which he would loan out for wedding feasts. He was always invited!

Near the end of Jesus's ministry, Jesus entered Jerusalem like a king, with crowds of people cheering. He went to the Temple, the heart of the nation, and challenged the authorities. That same week, on Thursday night, their reaction was put into motion. They would capture him. They would kill him. Jesus knew this was coming, so he gathered his closest companions to say goodbye. He gave them instructions. He also gave them a meal, a supper. It was the feast of Passover, when the Israelites would sacrifice a spotless lamb to remember how God's people had been rescued from Egypt back in the time of Moses.

> Jesus would die in place of the people who deserved to die, because they hadn't fulfilled the covenant. He would take their punishment and curse.

But in the middle of remembering, Jesus brought up something new. This supper was now his, he said, for a remembrance that would go far beyond the old one. He was the Lamb. He spoke of his body given for his own. He also spoke of his blood: "This cup is the new covenant between God and his people – an agreement confirmed with my blood, which is poured out as a sacrifice for you" (Luke 22:20; 1 Corinthians 11:25; see also Matthew 26:28; Mark 14:24). The new covenant would come through Jesus's death.

The phrase "blood of the covenant" comes from Exodus 24:8. The people, rescued from Egypt, were meeting with God at Mount Sinai. They had just been hearing instructions on how to live as God's people. Next the people were swearing their loyalty to the Lord. Animals were sacrificed and the blood divided, half for the people, half for the Lord. It was a symbol of taking an oath: "May my blood be shed just like this animal if I don't fulfil my commitment to you."

By the same blood symbol, God also swore his loyalty. He was ready to die for the people who belonged to him, to carry out his covenant commitment. Then, right after that oath ceremony, there was a feast. Moses and other leaders of the people climbed up the mountain, the mountain no one was allowed to even touch. Instead of dying in the holy presence of God with the brightness of his glory, they ate and drank (Exodus 24:11)!

When Jesus explained his supper to his dear ones, he used words from Exodus to make a connection. He was the one to be sacrificed, not an animal. He would die in place of the people who deserved to die, because they hadn't fulfilled the covenant. He would take their punishment and curse. That meant that now his covenant couldn't fail. And the result would be a feast as sinners eat together in the glorious presence of God.

Instead of an old, tired covenant, there was the promise of a covenant made new. The problem of sin would be dealt with once and for all.

This is already what is going on when we celebrate the supper Jesus left us. It will be much more glorious when he comes!

When Jesus talked about a "new covenant", he was connecting his death to the prophecy of Jeremiah 31 (which we already looked at a bit earlier). It was the awful time of the fall of Jerusalem, with a stubborn people hauled off as exiles to Babylon. Amid defeat, shame, and tears, God gave Jeremiah the message that the people losing everything would not be the end of the story. The people had not fulfilled the covenant they received from Abraham. They had not carried out their mission of living for God in his world, demonstrating what he is like. Curses, long promised, had come.

But God was still not going to walk away from his covenant commitment. His purpose of forming a people for himself, had not failed. Instead of an old, tired covenant, there was the promise of a covenant made new. The problem of sin would be dealt with once and for all. The problem of sinning too would be solved. It is a heart-level problem and has to be dealt with at that level. What God wants will be placed right inside of God's people: they will want him with their whole hearts.

This is the new covenant that Jesus declared in his supper. His death would bring at last the reality that hadn't come for more than 500 years after Jeremiah. Jesus was the one who had always understood and always wanted what God wants. In his death he would take on himself and absorb the power of sin at work in the world. He would be sacrificed in place of the people who broke covenant, who by their own oath deserved to die. And, by the Holy Spirit, what Jesus had done and was became real for those who belong to him.

New covenant is always found in Jesus. Baptism is a solemn commitment that joins us to Jesus, to his death and his resurrection. The Lord's Supper is a solemn feast, renewing covenant, joining us to Jesus afresh. We eat together, a people saved by his body and his blood, anticipating being together still more, with him and with others. By faith, baptism and the Lord's Supper connect us in covenant to Jesus and to God. This is how we, people from every race, language, culture, and nation, can hear God repeating to us: *You will be my people, and I will be your God.*

I think of that storekeeper who fled his home when his fearful neighbours listened to lies. They had decided he didn't belong. In church, however, he was welcomed and protected. His children were able to finish the school year in safety. And when things calmed down, they were all able to go back home.

Our new covenant connection in Jesus is the most important of all. We affirm this at our baptism, and every time we take the Lord's Supper. We know in the deepest parts of our soul that we are tied to him forever. And in that bond, we are indeed highly favoured.

Take time now to hear again and think over what Jeremiah says about the new covenant:

*"I have loved you, my people, with an everlasting love.
With unfailing love I have drawn you to myself."*

*. . . Now this is what the Lord says: "Sing with joy for Israel.
Shout for the greatest of nations!*

*Shout out with praise and joy: 'Save your people,
O Lord, the remnant of Israel!'" . . .*

*"The day is coming," says the Lord, "when I will make a new
covenant with the people of Israel and Judah. This covenant will
not be like the one I made with their ancestors when I took them
by the hand and brought them out of the land of Egypt.
They broke that covenant, though I loved them as a
husband loves his wife," says the Lord.*

*"But this is the new covenant I will make with the people of Israel
after those days," says the Lord. "I will put my instructions deep
within them, and I will write them on their hearts. I will be their
God, and they will be my people. And they will not need to teach
their neighbours, nor will they need to teach their relatives, saying,
'You should know the Lord.' For everyone, from the least to the
greatest, will know me already," says the Lord. "And I will forgive
their wickedness, and I will never again remember their sins."*

JEREMIAH 31:3, 7, 31-34

NINE

IT'S OUR STORY TOO

"Highly favoured!" Young Mary was stunned to hear the angel's words. Baffled. To be the virgin mother of God's Saviour!

Finally, she responded with willingness: "I am the Lord's servant. May everything you have said about me come true" (Luke 1:30-38). This would be a hard adventure for her. But it blesses us all to this day.

How about you? Have you heard God declare his favour over you? Do you need to hear it again? Have you felt the welcoming arms of his covenant? To be in Jesus? To know deep within that "my people" includes *you*, and to burst out in answer, "my God!"? What an adventure there is for you, for us together, to be swept into God's glorious story! It will be hard, but oh, so good. Scary, but joyous.

Right now, Noah is wondering what you will build. Abraham wants to see me march. Isaac asks what blessings we are passing on.

Maybe you are still baffled, overwhelmed, or unsure. Ask God to make you willing, eager to live and serve in covenant with him.

At the beginning of this book we talked about two surprises. The first was that in this world of sin and danger, we already have God's favour in Jesus. We are his people, and he is our God in the deep commitment of covenant. Second, this favour is better than we are used to thinking. It goes way beyond the feeble and flimsy things we ask for. It's a commitment that is unsettling, sometimes painful, and always wonderful.

Many of the themes in this book – the big story of God and his precious people – come together in two chapters almost at the end of the letter to the Hebrews.

Hebrews 11 begins with creation. By his word and power, God created a visible world in the middle of an invisible reality. Hebrews 12 concludes with trumpets, with the unshakeable kingdom of God in a new creation, after the old heavens and earth have been taken away.

In between, here we are! It's our big story. The last verse of Hebrews 11 says God had a better plan. He didn't want the heroes of faith, the long line marching through the old covenant from Abel onward (11:4-32), to "reach perfection without us" (11:40). Right now, Noah is wondering what you will build. Abraham wants to see me march. Isaac asks what blessings we are passing on. Joseph is eager for the sign of trust in God's promises you will leave in this world. Moses wants to see what privileges I will surrender in order to grab hold of God's people.

What obstacles will shrivel as together we step out to follow God? Rahab expects you to drop other identities for covenant loyalty. And so on, and so on. All of these covenant participants, God says, are waiting and watching. Their full reward in the new creation can't come yet. God has decided you and I need to be included in the blessings, too. The grand climax of all God's plans is for all of us together.

Who are your ancestors? For some people, ancestors are shadowy, hovering, manipulating spirits. For others they are simply long-ago dead people in the family. We might be curious, but we don't know much about them.

There is another way to use the term. Ancestors can be the people who have formed us. When we fail, we think about their disappointment and are ashamed. When we do what is right and hard and good, we think of their pride and we stand taller. These great ones in Hebrews 11 are ancestors for you and me.

The story continues (12:1): when it's our turn to run in the stadium of life, all our ancestors in the people of God are watching us, clapping their hands, and cheering. The story is unfinished until we do our part. Each one of us has our own individual race to run, but the victory is not an individual victory. It's ours. It belongs to the people of God. It is God's.

Our house is 50 meters from a football field. On weekend afternoons we may not be paying any attention to the match, but we know exactly when there is a goal or a near miss. The roar from the crowd and the groans make it plain. It is even louder for the players on the pitch.

Teams like to play before their home crowd. They run harder with the shouts of encouragement. Of course, in Hebrews 12 the picture is of a foot race, not a football match. In running, roars build as the finish line comes in sight. Runners find new strength and pound home.

Here, between creation and God's glorious conclusion, we live our lives running, focused on Jesus. He is "the champion who initiates and perfects our faith" (12:2), our beginning and our end. As we run in this life, we fix our eyes on him. We don't look at the crowd or talk to the crowd. If you turn to look at the other runners, you might stumble. Jesus is the one who counts. He is one who saw joy where other people could see only shame. He went to the cross and won. Jesus, by his blood, makes the new covenant. We are running to join him and all God's people and God himself (12:23-24).

Focusing on Jesus demands habits (life patterns) of prayer, of Scripture, of fellowship. We need to be reminded over and over again who Jesus is and what he cares about. We need to be reshaped by him. If I come to him only to get things I want, I never realize that the things I want are often puny and unimportant, or even downright wrong. But if I focus on him, it actually changes what I want.

Do I pray, "Lord help me write a great book"? Or do I pray, "Father, use these words to draw people to yourself, so they can be joyous, confident, and committed"?

In order to run well, we run light. We get rid of the things that slow us down. Sometimes those are sins, or maybe a hurt we hold on to rather than forgive. Other times, something good gets in our way. Is loyalty to your family more important than loyalty to Jesus?

In the big story in these two chapters in Hebrews, what stands out is "by faith, by faith, by faith". This isn't, "I believe that . . ." It isn't, "Yes, I think God exists." Neither is it some formula to get God to do what we want, where we say just the right words and chase away any doubting thought. No, it is trusting God, giving ourselves over to him and to what he wants.

Think about a chair, one of those bright, plastic ones that are everywhere. I can say, "I think it's strong enough to hold me up", as I stand and look at it on a shiny, polished floor. But I am only actually trusting the chair when I sit in it (and even lift my feet off the ground!). Faith means that what God says is real. And that shapes everything we do, even when these things seem far away and small to us right now.

Noah built a huge ship without seeing the ocean (11:7). Abraham spent his whole life as a nomad living in tents, content that God would give him a permanent city he never saw (11:8-11). He was even ready to sacrifice his only son, trusting that a huge people would somehow be born from that same son (11:17-19).

You might decide that you should confront dangerous patterns in your family. You might reach out with God's Good News to a neglected group of people. You might decide there is far more in the Bible than you ever realized, that it is worth the hard work of careful reading and slow study.

And let's be clear: By faith there were victories. By that same faith there were defeats. God decides – our loving covenant God. By trusting God, his servants were used to conquer kingdoms, to establish justice, to see promises come true, to shut the mouths of lions, to put out raging flames (11:33-34). Yay! Dead people were brought back to life (11:35)!

But in the same verse, others chose to die and wait for the final resurrection. There is no difference in the faith of those who see wonders accomplished and those who suffer, are oppressed, and are rejected (11:36-39). The people of God live by the power of God in a world that doesn't want him. Sometimes that power is shown by huge successes. Sometimes it is shown by enabling us to endure what is unspeakable and ghastly.

We have friends who went to live in a village with 500 Muslim families and no followers of Jesus. They learned the language and got to know people. They told stories from the Bible. They told about Jesus. After 8 years, 11 people were baptized, declaring their covenant with Jesus. And just weeks later, our friends had to leave with a terrible illness, a spreading paralysis that steals the body's ability to stand, to speak, to chew, and eventually to breath. Huge success – as well as the unspeakable and ghastly.

> Sometimes that power is shown by huge successes. Sometimes it is shown by enabling us to endure what is unspeakable and ghastly.

In this time between creation and final glory, it is no surprise to have a hard time. It is actually one of the privileges of belonging to God. He is committed to what is "good for us, so that we might share in his holiness" (12:10). He shows himself to be a demanding Father, loving us enough to discipline us and correct us. The hard training hurts but builds up our strength in doing right (12:11). This means difficulties are no reason to give up or go back. Nor should we despise God's promises (12:16).

These realities of new creation and new covenant have already begun. Did you notice what it says in Hebrews 12:22: "You have come to Mount Zion, to the city of the living God, the heavenly Jerusalem, and to countless thousands of angels in a joyful gathering." It is written, "you have come", not "you will come"! The kingdom that cannot be shaken is something that "we are receiving" now (12:28). The reality of belonging to God and living in his presence in Jesus has already begun. The glory and the honour we have now are real, right here in this earth (even while more is coming).

So, this is how we should live. Highly favoured in this world, it's our turn to live by faith, to work, and to delight. God in the beginning. God in the middle. God in the end. "You will be my people, and I will be your God."

POSTSCRIPT

A VERY BIG QUESTI

I need to ask you something important.

All through this book I've assumed that you and I are t
together, that we, together, are part of the people of God. I
be you are not really sure. Maybe you have been nodding you
thinking "I guess so. It could be." Maybe you thought it was er
to belong to a church, or even to have your parents belong
church. Maybe you thought following the practices of the mosq
was enough.

But now you realize something else needs to come first. You
sense the need to belong to God, to be bound to him. And that
happens in Jesus.

Where do you stand with Jesus?

We were made for honour by God, to rule his world, represent-
ing him. Instead we have turned away from God in sin and shame,
trying to rule ourselves and everything and everyone around us for
ourselves. In our deepest hearts we have rejected God. We have
despised him. Our lives, our families, our communities, our countries, our world – all of it is deeply messed up by every person's
heart commitment to rebellion that the Bible calls sin. We are
twisted away from God.

Yet God has turned towards us. His Son, Jesus, has come looking for us. He has actually become one of us. We need to turn
around, to turn to Jesus, to turn back to God.

Have you turned to Jesus, away from yourself and your sin?

sent Jesus to do what we cannot do. We cannot rescue our-
We cannot put ourselves right with God. We cannot take away
fense and the hurt. We cannot undo the power of death that
us all in futility. When Jesus willingly died, stretched out on a
in agony, he did it for us, taking our place. It was our fair pun-
nent, what we deserved. When God raised Jesus from the dead,
declared the sacrifice made and the mission accomplished.

The eternal life of the new creation has been launched. For those
ho trust Jesus, for those who lean on him, saying, "My Saviour,
my Lord!", there is forgiveness, there is new life, there is covenant
belonging.

Have you trusted Jesus as your Saviour, your Lord? Do you trust
him as standing in your place so you can stand in him, in the presence of God?

God's Spirit is alive and active in this world. I haven't talked
much about the Holy Spirit in this book, but he is the one who
breathed out the very words of Scripture through the prophets and
apostles. He demonstrates their truth through acts of power. He
pours rich gifts for service on God's people. He takes the reality of
who Jesus is and grips us with it, turning our lives around, so that
God's new life bursts into us and spreads all through us. He links
us up with others of God's people who can pray for us, counsel us,
teach us, and walk with us.

If you want to follow Jesus in a new way, pray. In your own
words, tell him you are sorry for rejecting him, and ask for forgiveness. Explain that you want to belong to God's people. You can
express yourself honestly to Jesus, just as if you are talking to someone sitting next to you. Ask God's Holy Spirit to show you, to grip
you, and to guide you.

Find a follower of Jesus you can respect to help you turn around
and commit yourself to trust Jesus. Find a church to belong to, where
you can live as part of God's covenant people. This is your time to
decide to follow the Lord Jesus. Come on, let's go together!

Bible Study
Guide

TWO SURPRISES

We already have God's favour, and it is both better and harder than we imagine. This passage is a very personal promise of favour. Before reading it, pray and ask for God's guidance.

JEREMIAH 1:17-19

> ¹⁷ "Get up and prepare for action.
>   Go out and tell them everything I tell you to say.
> Do not be afraid of them,
>   or I will make you look foolish in front of them.
> ¹⁸ For see, today I have made you strong
>   like a fortified city that cannot be captured,
>   like an iron pillar or a bronze wall.
> You will stand against the whole land—
>   the kings, officials, priests, and people of Judah.
> ¹⁹ They will fight you, but they will fail.
>   For I am with you, and I will look after you.
>   I, the Lord, have spoken!"

God is giving Jeremiah a job to do which Jeremiah doesn't think he can handle.

1. What work is Jeremiah going to do (Jeremiah 1:17)?
2. Do you think it was going to be an easy job?
   What are the clues you see in each one of these three verses?
   It is one thing to "stand against" kings. It is another to stand against the whole people. Which do you think would be harder for you?

3. What makes the difference for Jeremiah (1:19)?
   How can he possibly do what God tells him to do?
4. Does the promise "I am with you and I will look after
   you" sound like Jeremiah had God's favour?
   Do you want God to say that to you?
   What if it means being given something very hard?
5. When we belong to Jesus, we already have God's favour,
   and it can be better and harder than we imagine. Which
   of these two surprises is the bigger one for you? Why?

Of course, just like Jeremiah, we don't get one surprise without the
other. They come together. Don't be afraid! After all, "I, the Lord,
have spoken!" Talk to God about it in prayer.

TWO

THE BIG STORY

The whole story of the Bible, from Genesis to Revelation, from creation to new creation, is what helps us make sense of every part. This passage tells one small story about Jesus and his disciples. But it only makes sense if we remember Genesis 1 and 2, the stories of King David, God's promises for the future, and God's big story. The big story keeps breaking in. Before reading it, pray and ask for God's guidance.

LUKE 6:1-5

¹ One Sabbath day as Jesus was walking through some grainfields, his disciples broke off heads of grain, rubbed off the husks in their hands, and ate the grain. ² But some Pharisees said, "Why are you breaking the law by harvesting grain on the Sabbath?" ³ Jesus replied, "Haven't you read in the Scriptures what David did when he and his companions were hungry? ⁴ He went into the house of God and broke the law by eating the sacred loaves of bread that only the priests can eat. He also gave some to his companions." ⁵ And Jesus added, "The Son of Man is Lord, even over the Sabbath."

1. "Sabbath" is not a word we use very much in ordinary speech. It comes from a Hebrew word meaning "rest". The idea of having a "sabbath" started in Genesis 2. When God made the world, he "rested" on the seventh day. Why is it important that this event happened on the Sabbath (Luke 6:1)?
2. Jesus brings up an old story from 1 Samuel 21. Why do you think he talks about David and his companions

when his own companions were being accused?

At that time, God had promised that David would be king, but he was not king yet. David was running for his life! Is there something similar in Jesus' situation? What?

3. What does Jesus call himself (Luke 1:5)?

What do you think the title "Son of Man" means? (It was not an ordinary way to talk about someone.)

4. What does Jesus say about himself (1:5)?

Who had first made the Sabbath?

What do you think this seems to say about who Jesus is?

5. When do you think Jesus will give his people rest?

Have you already begun to find real rest in Jesus?

Talk to him about the rest you have, and the rest you need.

THREE

ONE POWERFUL SENTENCE

"You will be my people; I will be your God" links the Bible from end to end. It strengthens us in every situation of our lives. This passage echoes the same language but addresses another situation: What about when we feel we are doing everything God wants? When, in fact, we think God owes us something? It may be that God has a complaint. Before reading it, pray and ask for God's guidance.

PSALM 50:7-15

> [7] "O my people, listen as I speak.
>   Here are my charges against you, O Israel:
>   I am God, your God!
> [8] I have no complaint about your sacrifices
>   or the burnt offerings you constantly offer.
> [9] But I do not need the bulls from your barns
>   or the goats from your pens.
> [10] For all the animals of the forest are mine,
>   and I own the cattle on a thousand hills.
> [11] I know every bird on the mountains,
>   and all the animals of the field are mine.
> [12] If I were hungry, I would not tell you,
>   for all the world is mine and everything in it.
> [13] Do I eat the meat of bulls?
>   Do I drink the blood of goats?
> [14] Make thankfulness your sacrifice to God,
>   and keep the vows you made to the Most High.

¹⁵ Then call on me when you are in trouble,
   and I will rescue you,
   and you will give me glory."

1. How does the key phrase "You will be my people; I will be
   your God" show up here (Psalm 50:7)?
   How is it different this time from when it was used to
   comfort God's people?
2. What does God **not** complain about (50:8)?
   In the time of the Old Testament, worshipping God
   included presenting animals to him as a sacrifice. How
   had the people of Israel gotten it wrong here?
   What do you think God **does** want to complain about in
   this psalm?
3. How does God want his people to change (50:14)?
4. What promise does he make (50:15)?
   It's wonderful to be rescued from trouble. What is even
   bigger and better than that, coming at the very end of
   verse 15?
5. When we belong to God in Jesus, when he says to us, "You
   are mine", that gives him a right to complain about us.
   What do you think God would complain about to you?
   Are there things you do that make you think God owes
   you something? That you are paying him somehow?
   What changes should you make?

Pray and remember his promise: When you are in trouble, I will
rescue you **and** you will give me glory.

FOUR

ONE POWERFUL WORD

Covenant is key. Hard to understand, it is the foundation between us and God. This passage keeps coming back to "covenant", but this one here is between people, not with God. Before reading it, pray and ask for God's guidance.

GENESIS 31:43-54

> ⁴³ Then Laban replied to Jacob, "These women are my daughters, these children are my grandchildren, and these flocks are my flocks—in fact, everything you see is mine. But what can I do now about my daughters and their children? ⁴⁴ So come, let's make a covenant, you and I, and it will be a witness to our commitment."
> ⁴⁵ So Jacob took a stone and set it up as a monument.
> ⁴⁶ Then he told his family members, "Gather some stones." So they gathered stones and piled them in a heap. Then Jacob and Laban sat down beside the pile of stones to eat a covenant meal. ⁴⁷ To commemorate the event, Laban called the place Jegar-sahadutha (which means "witness pile" in Aramaic), and Jacob called it Galeed (which means "witness pile" in Hebrew).
> ⁴⁸ Then Laban declared, "This pile of stones will stand as a witness to remind us of the covenant we have made today." This explains why it was called Galeed— "Witness Pile." ⁴⁹ But it was also called Mizpah (which means "watchtower"), for Laban said, "May the Lord keep watch between us to make sure that we keep this covenant when we are out of each other's sight.

[50] If you mistreat my daughters or if you marry other wives, God will see it even if no one else does. He is a witness to this covenant between us.
[51] "See this pile of stones," Laban continued, "and see this monument I have set between us. [52] They stand between us as witnesses of our vows. I will never pass this pile of stones to harm you, and you must never pass these stones or this monument to harm me. [53] I call on the God of our ancestors—the God of your grandfather Abraham and the God of my grandfather Nahor—to serve as a judge between us."
So Jacob took an oath before the fearsome God of his father, Isaac, to respect the boundary line. [54] Then Jacob offered a sacrifice to God there on the mountain and invited everyone to a covenant feast. After they had eaten, they spent the night on the mountain.

1. How many times can you find that one powerful word, *covenant*, in these verses?
2. For years Jacob and his father-in-law, Laban, have been tricking each other. Each one has taken advantage of the other. Now it almost comes to blows – family killing family. But God has intervened. What do Jacob and Laban do instead of fighting?
3. What things do you notice that go along with making a covenant:
   . . . in verse 44? How does having a witness help? Is a stone by itself a witness? Who is the more important witness (31:50)?
   . . . in verse 45? What is the stone monument for?
   . . . in verse 46? Why is sitting down to eat together important?
   . . . in verse 53? What do they ask God to do about their covenant?

4. Is there a conflict in your family that could be helped by a covenant?
5. Is there a conflict in your country that could be helped by a covenant?

Pray, asking for God's solutions to these conflicts, and for confidence about what you should do.

FIVE

FOUR MARKS OF A COVENANT

When God makes covenant with us, the relationship is exclusive, secure, demanding, and full of purpose. In this passage, God talks to his people and tells us about the relationship. Before reading it, pray and ask for God's guidance.

Isaiah 43:1-4

¹ But now, O Jacob, listen to the Lord who created you.
O Israel, the one who formed you says,
"Do not be afraid, for I have ransomed you.
I have called you by name; you are mine.
² When you go through deep waters,
I will be with you.
When you go through rivers of difficulty,
you will not drown.
When you walk through the fire of oppression,
you will not be burned up;
the flames will not consume you.
³ For I am the Lord, your God,
the Holy One of Israel, your Saviour.
I gave Egypt as a ransom for your freedom;
I gave Ethiopia and Seba in your place.
⁴ Others were given in exchange for you.
I traded their lives for yours
because you are precious to me.
You are honoured, and I love you."

God has been punishing his people for their stubborn refusal to listen to him.

1. What change is coming now (Isaiah 43:1)?
   Why shouldn't we be afraid?
   What does the word *ransom* mean?
   How do you feel when God knows your true name and tells you, "You are mine"?
2. Does God promise his people no problems (43:2)?
   What does he say that is even better than that?
3. The Lord calls himself "your God" (covenant language!).
   What else does he call himself (43:3)?
4. God has handed powerful nations over to defeat but will rescue little Israel (43:3). This astonishing exchange points to an even bigger ransom that is coming. Who has he given for your life and your sin?
5. What signs do you see in these verses that the relationship between God and his people is:
   exclusive?
   secure?
   demanding?
   full of purpose?

In covenant, we are precious, honoured, and loved (43:4). You are precious, honoured, and loved! Tell God how that changes you today.

SIX

WHAT A COVENANT LOOKS LIKE

God created marriage to show us covenant. Marriage describes our relationship with him.

This passage shows Paul getting very passionate about the marriage between Jesus and his people in Corinth. Before reading it, pray and ask for God's guidance.

2 Corinthians 11:1-4

> ¹ I hope you will put up with a little more of my foolishness. Please bear with me. ² For I am jealous for you with the jealousy of God himself. I promised you as a pure bride to one husband—Christ. ³ But I fear that somehow your pure and undivided devotion to Christ will be corrupted, just as Eve was deceived by the cunning ways of the serpent. ⁴ You happily put up with whatever anyone tells you, even if they preach a different Jesus than the one we preach, or a different kind of Spirit than the one you received, or a different kind of gospel than the one you believed.

Preaching, teaching, praying, Paul had seen God start a church in the bustling port city of Corinth. Instead of idols, people were worshipping the one true God and following Jesus as Lord and Saviour. But there were lots of problems. After Paul left, he wrote letters and sent messengers, trying to sort things out. But other people showed up, too, with different ideas. Some of them had some very harsh things to say about Paul himself.

1. What does Paul ask the church to do (2 Corinthians 11:1)? Why would he need to ask something like that?
2. Then Paul uses a startling word – twice. What is it (11:2)? Isn't jealousy a sin? How can God be jealous? When could jealousy not be wrong?
3. What comparison does Paul use to explain his jealousy (11:2)? Who is the bride and who is the husband? Have you seen this picture other places in the Bible? Where?
4. What is Paul concerned about (11:3)? What should a bride have? What might happen to this one?
5. What is the sign that pure, undivided devotion is under threat (11:4)? Are there things you "happily put up with" that make you disloyal to Jesus? How can you be sure you are following the real Jesus, the real Spirit, the real gospel?
6. Do you make Jesus jealous? How can you stop?

Tell him how his love makes you feel and what you are going to do about it.

SEVEN

DOES THE COVENANT PREVENT SUFFERING?

From the Psalms and Job, this chapter wrestles with being God's covenant people and suffering at the same time. In this passage, the apostle Peter tackles the same problem head on. Before reading it, pray and ask for God's guidance.

1 Peter 4:12-19

[12] Dear friends, don't be surprised at the fiery trials you are going through, as if something strange were happening to you. [13] Instead, be very glad—for these trials make you partners with Christ in his suffering, so that you will have the wonderful joy of seeing his glory when it is revealed to all the world.

[14] If you are insulted because you bear the name of Christ, you will be blessed, for the glorious Spirit of God rests upon you. [15] If you suffer, however, it must not be for murder, stealing, making trouble, or prying into other people's affairs. [16] But it is no shame to suffer for being a Christian. Praise God for the privilege of being called by his name! [17] For the time has come for judgement, and it must begin with God's household. And if judgement begins with us, what terrible fate awaits those who have never obeyed God's Good News? [18] And also,

"If the righteous are barely saved,
what will happen to godless sinners?"
[19] So if you are suffering in a manner that pleases God,
keep on doing what is right, and trust your lives to the
God who created you, for he will never fail you.

1. The apostle Peter writes to "Dear friends".
   What does he say we shouldn't do (1 Peter 4:12)?
   What reason does he give?
   How does surprise make it harder for us to go through
   "fiery trials"?
2. What should we do instead of being surprised at trials
   (4:13)?
   Why?
   How is that possible?
3. Peter then gives an example of suffering. What is it (4:14)?
   What is a good reason for suffering? (See 4:16 as well.)
   What are bad reasons for suffering (4:15)?
4. When Peter starts talking about judgement, what does he
   call us (4:17)?
   Yes, we are God's very own family by covenant! What
   privilege does that give us?
   Does it mean we are exempted from trouble?
5. What is Peter's final recommendation (4:19)?
   What promise does he give?
6. Is there a hardship or suffering surprising you right now?
   How can you go through it in a way that pleases God?
   Peter calls us "partners with Christ" as well as God's
   family – covenant language. How does what you have
   learned about God's covenant favour make you stronger?
   Who could you tell about it?

Tell God how you feel and what you will do.

EIGHT

TIED FOREVER TO JESUS

By baptism and the Lord's Supper we declare we are in Jesus. In this passage Paul talks about himself and what belonging to Jesus means. Before reading it, pray, asking God's guidance.

PHILIPPIANS 3:7-11

> [7] I once thought these things were valuable, but now I consider them worthless because of what Christ has done. [8] Yes, everything else is worthless when compared with the infinite value of knowing Christ Jesus my Lord. For his sake I have discarded everything else, counting it all as rubbish, so that I could gain Christ [9] and become one with him. I no longer count on my own righteousness through obeying the law; rather, I become righteous through faith in Christ. For God's way of making us right with himself depends on faith. [10] I want to know Christ and experience the mighty power that raised him from the dead. I want to suffer with him, sharing in his death, [11] so that one way or another I will experience the resurrection from the dead!

Paul, the apostle, has been talking about the things he used to do, used to have, and used to count on. Things like his background, his faithful religion, and his eager action for God. He thought these things gave him honour and made God pleased with him.

1. What does Paul say he thinks now about these things (Philippians 3:7)?
   What has changed? What makes the difference for him?
2. What is the comparison Paul makes (3:8)?
   Do you think Paul would see those things like you do?
3. What does Paul say he wants more than anything else (end of 3:8 and beginning of 3:9)?
   Why does he want it so much?
4. Notice Paul's connection to Jesus: gaining him, becoming one with him, really knowing him (3:8, 9, 10). This is intense belonging and covenant language. What is Paul looking forward to now (3:10)?
   Does Paul expect to experience mighty death-defeating power without suffering?
5. Pause and quiet your heart. As you answer these next questions, be honest, even if your answer isn't a good Christian answer. Consider how you spend your time and what you talk about.
   What would you say you value most? What do you want more than anything else?
   What do you treat as "rubbish" or less important?
   How much does belonging to Jesus matter?
   Is your trust in him?

Tell God what belonging to Jesus means to you.

NINE

IT'S OUR STORY TOO

This last chapter of the book focuses on our story, lived out inside God's story, dwelling on chapters 11 and 12 of Hebrews. This passage puts us right in the middle of that grand sweep from the very beginning to the very end. Before reading it, pray and ask for God's guidance.

Hebrews 12:1-4

> ¹ Therefore, since we are surrounded by such a huge crowd of witnesses to the life of faith, let us strip off every weight that slows us down, especially the sin that so easily trips us up. And let us run with endurance the race God has set before us. ² We do this by keeping our eyes on Jesus, the champion who initiates and perfects our faith. Because of the joy awaiting him, he endured the cross, disregarding its shame. Now he is seated in the place of honour beside God's throne. ³ Think of all the hostility he endured from sinful people; then you won't become weary and give up. ⁴ After all, you have not yet given your lives in your struggle against sin.

1. When you think of God's faithful ones through history watching you, who comes especially to mind (Hebrews 12:1)?
   Maybe someone from the Bible?
   Maybe someone you have known?
2. What weight is slowing you down as you run the long race of life for God?

3. What sin is about to trip you up?
4. What can you do today to keep looking to Jesus, to focus on him (12:2)?
5. What two things does Jesus do for our faith (12:2)? How does that make you feel?
6. Are you feeling weary, like giving up (12:3)? Is there some shame in your life that makes following Jesus seem too hard?

Jesus fought sin and won. We have come to him, to his glory and his unshakeable kingdom. Deep joy and rich honour are what he gives us. We are highly favoured! He is taking care of us. Thank God that you are his beloved child. Your story will have hard parts and good parts. Best of all, it is part of his story. And that means a happy ending!